POCKET

GLASGOW

Neil Wilson

Top: Duke of Wellington statue (p86),
Royal Exchange Square
Bottom: People's Palace (p63),
Glasgow Green

Contents

Plan Your Trip 4

The Journey Begins Here 4
Our Picks 6
Perfect Days 20
Get Prepared 24
When To Go 26
Getting There 28
Getting Around 29
A Few Surprises 32

Explore Glasgow 35

Central Glasgow 37
East End 55
Merchant City 71
Southside & the Clyde 95
West End 117

Glasgow Toolkit 143

Family Travel 144
Accommodation 145
Food, Drink & Nightlife 146
LGBTIQ+ Travel 148
Health & Safe Travel 149
Responsible Travel 150
Accessible Travel 152
Nuts & Bolts 153
Index 154

★ Top Experiences

Mackintosh at the Willow 40
Glasgow Cathedral 57
St Mungo Museum 60
Glasgow Necropolis 61
City Chambers 74
Sharmanka Kinetic Theatre 78
George Square 80
Gallery of Modern Art 81
Burrell Collection 98
Riverside Museum 102
Glasgow Science Centre 104
House for an Art Lover 106
Kelvingrove Art Gallery 120
Hunterian Museum 124
Hunterian Art Gallery 126
Mackintosh House 126

FROM TOP LEFT: VICKI_SMITH/SHUTTERSTOCK ©, KENSOFTTH/SHUTTERSTOCK ©

The Journey Begins Here

Sporting a disarming blend of sophistication and down-to-earth humour, Scotland's biggest city has evolved over the last few decades to become one of Britain's most intriguing metropolises. The handsome Victorian buildings, legacies of wealth generated from manufacturing and trade, suggest a staid sort of place. Very wrong. Glasgow's streets are packed with stylish bars, inventive restaurants and one of the UK's best live-music scenes. Whether you're looking for Italian fashion or preloved denim, its shopping is legendary, and there are world-class museums and galleries which also showcase the city's industrial heritage.

Neil Wilson
@neil3965
Born and raised in Glasgow, Neil is a travel writer who now lives in Perthshire and has covered Scotland for Lonely Planet for more than 25 years.

Kelvingrove Art Gallery & Museum (p120)
ULMUS MEDIA/SHUTTERSTOCK ©

4

THE BEST

Food Experiences

Glasgow is the best foodie city in Scotland, with a stupendous range of restaurants and cafes. The West End is a culinary centre, with the Merchant City also boasting a high concentration of quality establishments.

Sample the finest of Scottish cuisine at **The Ubiquitous Chip**, a pioneer of locally sourced produce that's been around since 1971. (p132)

Treat yourself to an indulgent champagne afternoon tea amid the Victorian splendour of the Merchant City's **Corinthian Club**. (pictured; p91)

Enjoy Glasgow's, and Scotland's, most popular dish (not haggis, but chicken tikka masala) at the restaurant where it was invented: **Shish Mahal**. (p135)

Tuck into the best of sustainable Scottish seafood in the relaxed, nautical-themed setting of **The Finnieston**. (pictured; p138)

Join the University of Glasgow students soothing their hangovers with fried egg and chips at the **University Cafe**. (p137)

Right: University Cafe (p137)

THE BEST

Nightlife Experiences

Glaswegians are known to enjoy a beverage or two, and some of Britain's best nightlife is found in the din and sometimes roar of the city's pubs, clubs and bars.

Take a guided **whisky tour** and discover some of the West End's best bars while you learn about Scotland's national drink. (p135)

Enjoy a pint of real ale (or two) in the gleaming mahogany-and-mirrors surroundings of **The Horse Shoe Bar**, one of Glasgow's oldest and most popular pubs. (p53)

Sip a cocktail beneath the red-brick railway vaults of Central Station at **Platform** before hitting the dance floor at the **New World** club. (p49)

Join the Saturday-night crowds of revellers thronging the city centre bars in a **pub crawl along Bath Street**. (p47)

Listen to the newest of Glasgow's up-and-coming bands at the time-honoured live-music venue **King Tut's Wah Wah Hut**. (pictured; p50)

Right: Bath Street (p47)

THE BEST

Entertainment Experiences

Glasgow is Scotland's entertainment capital, from classical music, theatre and ballet to an astonishing range of live-music venues. To tap into the scene, check out What's On Glasgow (*whatsonglasgow.co.uk*), an invaluable free events guide.

Enjoy lunchtime theatre, an idea that Glasgow has embraced in a big way since its introduction in 2004 – **A Play, A Pie and A Pint** at Oràn Mór is now a city institution. (p138)

Laugh your way through a comedy gig at **The Stand**, in a city that has provided the world with a host of much-loved comedians. (pictured; p136)

Learn all about Glasgow's varied and fascinating musical heritage while strolling the streets with **Glasgow Music City Tours**. (p89)

Settle in for an evening of sublime classical music after booking tickets for an orchestral performance at the **City Halls**. (pictured; p87)

Get ready to yell 'Oh yes she is.' as part of the inevitable audience participation at a **Pavilion Theatre** Christmas pantomime. (p46)

Right: Pavilion Theatre (p46)

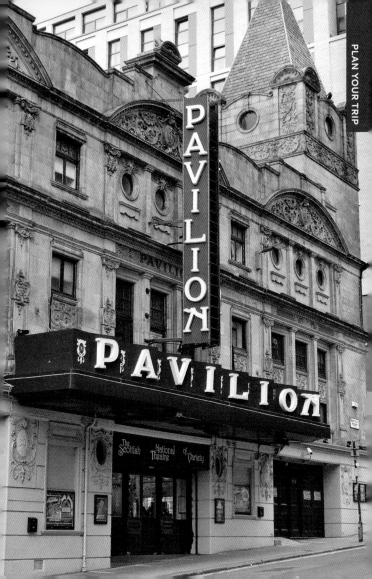

THE BEST

Museum Experiences

Collecting was big in Victorian times when Glasgow was overflowing with merchant wealth, so it's no surprise that the city's architectural legacy from the period is complemented by some wonderful museums.

Admire the modern architecture and waterfront setting of Zaha Hadid's **Riverside Museum** before exploring the historic transport treasures within. (p102)

Roam the hallowed halls of the University of Glasgow's superb **Hunterian Museum**, a Victorian collection cleverly curated and presented for the present day. (pictured; p124)

Discover the history of Glasgow's world-beating shipbuilding industry at **Fairfield Heritage**. (p111)

Enter a lovingly preserved time capsule of Edwardian middle-class life at the **Tenement House**. (p47)

Ponder the mysteries of life, love and death through the prism of the world's great religions at **St Mungo Museum of Religious Life & Art**. (pictured; p60)

Investigate the world's first city police force at **Glasgow Police Museum**, and have a chat with retired officers. (p86)

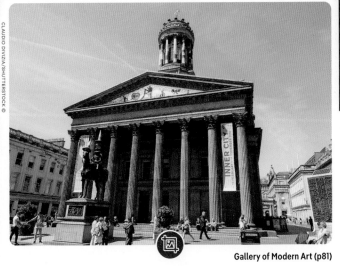

Gallery of Modern Art (p81)

THE BEST

Art-Viewing Experiences

Art has long played an important part in the city's cultural life, from the collections of wealthy industrialists, to the Glasgow artists whose works hang both here and around the world.

Admire the amazing breadth of interest reflected in the eclectic displays of the important **Burrell Collection**. (p98)

Get up close to European masterpieces, including Salvador Dalí's *Christ of St John of the Cross*, at **Kelvingrove Art Gallery & Museum**. (p120)

Acquaint yourself with the works of the Glasgow Boys and Girls, the Scottish Colourists and James McNeill Whistler at the **Hunterian Art Gallery**. (p126)

Challenge your preconceptions about what does and doesn't constitute a work of art while browsing the exhibitions at the **Gallery of Modern Art**. (p81)

Take a guided tour of the **City Chambers** to see masterpieces by EA Hornel, magnificent murals by the Glasgow Boys and some brilliant portraits of past Lord Provosts. (p74)

Outdoors Experiences

Glasgow's nickname of the 'Dear Green Place' is warranted by the city's many parks and gardens – places to escape from the hustle and bustle of the streets, to enjoy a picnic lunch and to walk or cycle away your cares.

Take to the water on a **Seaforce Powerboats** tour from the jetty at Riverside Museum and see the city from a different perspective. (p110)

Amble amid the palms and tropical plants in the gorgeous Kibble Palace glasshouse at the West End's **Botanic Gardens**. (pictured; p132)

Hire a bike and ride the Clyde Walkway to **Cuningar Loop**, where you can test your climbing skills at the outdoor bouldering park. (pictured; p112)

Board the historic paddle steamer **PS Waverley** for a nostalgic cruise down the Firth of Clyde to the islands of Cumbrae, Bute and Arran. (p112)

Keep a lookout for squirrels as you hike the woodland trails around **Pollok Country Park**. (p98)

Combine healthy exercise with art appreciation by following the **City Centre Mural Trail**. (p87)

Right: PS Waverly (p112)

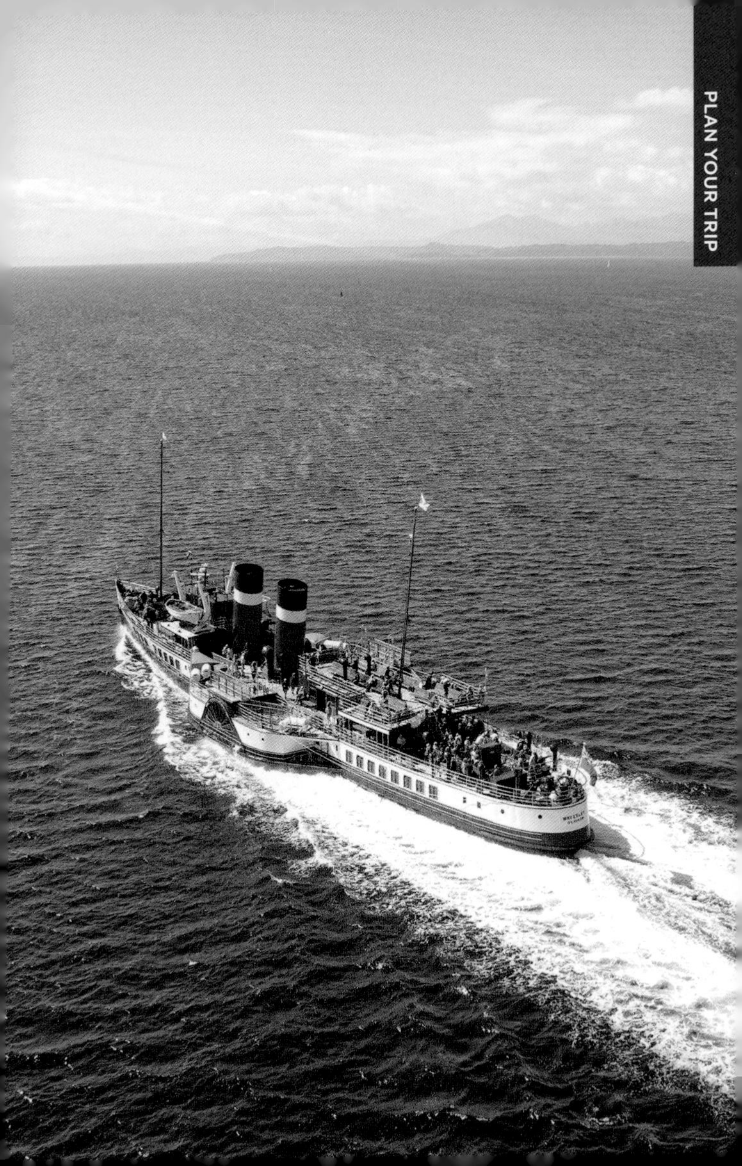

THE BEST

Historical Experiences

Glasgow's history is written in stone, from the ancient carved grave slabs of Govan and the Gothic majesty of its medieval cathedral to the Victorian monuments of the Necropolis and its university spire.

Gaze on the Govan Stones, beautifully carved relics of the ancient kingdom of Strathclyde. (p110)

Immerse yourself in the medieval splendour of Glasgow Cathedral and its venerable vaults. (p57)

Wander the Victorian monuments of the Glasgow Necropolis graveyard and soak up the city views. (p61)

Appreciate the wonderful contributions Glasgow has made to the advancement of medical science at the Friends of Glasgow Royal Infirmary Museum. (p67)

Take a stroll around the quadrangles of the University of Glasgow's Gilbert Scott Building, and grab an Insta-worthy image amid the forest of Gothic vaults and columns in the cloister. (p133)

Glasgow Necropolis (p61)

TAKASHI IMAGES/SHUTTERSTOCK ©

THE BEST

Architecture & Design Experiences

The work of Charles Rennie Mackintosh gives Glasgow an instant appeal for lovers of architecture and design with his legacy spread across the city, while the Victorian grandeur of the city centre provides a dignified background.

Visit **House for an Art Lover** to marvel at this modern realisation of a Mackintosh design never completed in his lifetime. (pictured; p106)

Join a guided tour of **Mackintosh at the Willow** to appreciate the originality and attention to detail of Glasgow's favourite architect. (p40)

Climb the stairs of the **Mackintosh House** to find this stunning recreation of the home he once shared with his wife Margaret Macdonald. (p126)

Learn about the achievements of Alexander Thomson, Glasgow's other great architect, at his domestic masterpiece **Holmwood House**. (p110)

Don't forget to look up as you walk the streets of the **Merchant City** or you'll miss the many impressive and ornate Victorian facades that testify to Glasgow's imperial wealth. (pictured; p71)

JEFF J MITCHELL/GETTY IMAGES ©

World Pipe Band Championships (p66)

THE BEST

Festival Experiences

Edinburgh may be known as Scotland's festival city, but Glasgow runs it a close second with a packed programme throughout the year. From comedy to *ceilidhs*, popular music to massed pipe bands, there's an event to suit everyone.

Warm yourself in the depths of a Scottish winter with the toe-tapping trad, folk and roots music of **Celtic Connections**. (p89)

Giggle or groan through a cornucopia of comedians from all over the globe at the **Glasgow International Comedy Festival**. (p136)

Dive into the world of the silver screen and attend a selection of film premieres at the **Glasgow Film Festival**. (p48)

Indulge yourself in a feast of music, theatre, comedy and visual art at **WestFest**, with a programme that runs for the entire month of June. (p135)

Cast aside your doubts and join the crowds jigging to the skirl of the bagpipes at the **World Pipe Band Championships**. (p66)

Best for Kids

Climb aboard Victorian trams, massive steam locomotives and a 19th-century tall ship at the **Riverside Museum** (p102).

Watch your youngsters explore the soft play area at **Glasgow Science Centre** while older kids expand their minds with the interactive exhibits (p104).

Enter a realm of the imagination amid the strange and wonderful creations at **Sharmanka Kinetic Theatre** (p78).

Go wild in **Kelvingrove Park** and have fun in the play areas, climbing frames and skate park (p134).

Run onto Scotland's national football pitch to the recorded roar of the crowd as part of a stadium tour at **Hampden Park** (p111).

Best for Free

Witness some of the world's greatest works of art assembled in one place at the awe-inspiring **Burrell Collection** (p98).

Soak up the colour and spectacle of **The Barras** weekend market, and maybe grab a few bargains too (p66).

Roam the galleries of magnificent **Kelvingrove Art Gallery & Museum** and enjoy a free lunchtime organ recital (p120).

Wander at will through the medieval maze of **Glasgow Cathedral** and learn about its history from volunteer guides (p57).

Marvel at the splendour and expense lavished on the **City Chambers** (Glasgow's city hall) on a free guided tour of the building (p74).

Perfect Days

Whether you've got one day in Glasgow or more, make the most of your time with this selection of experiences that are not to be missed.

Glasgow Cathedral (p57)

━━━ DAY ONE ━━━

Only Have One Day?

MORNING
Start by visiting **Glasgow Cathedral** (p57) and the hillside **Glasgow Necropolis** (pictured; p61). Then drop into **St Mungo Museum of Religious Life & Art** (p60) and nose around **Provand's Lordship** (p66), Glasgow's oldest house. Stroll down to Merchant City for lunch.

AFTERNOON
Head across the river to Pollok Country Park and spend the entire afternoon browsing the magnificent **Burrell Collection** (p98). Afterwards, wander the park's leafy trails before returning to the city centre.

EVENING
After a sumptuous dinner at **Glaschu** (p90), see a show at the **Pavilion Theatre** (p46) or a classical concert at **City Halls** (p87), or hit **Bar Gandolfi** (p91) for cocktails. This is also the heart of Glasgow's **LGBTIQ+ nightlife**, with several venues.

A Weekend Trip

MORNING

Perk up with coffee at **Riverhill Coffee Bar** (p51) then take stroll to **the Barras** (p66) weekend market for a taste of the real Glasgow. Return to Buchanan St, popping into **Argyll Arcade** (pictured; p92) and **Princes Square** (p92). Meander westward for lunch at **Mackintosh at the Willow** (p40).

AFTERNOON

Head to **Kelvingrove Art Gallery & Museum** (p120) and spend the afternoon marvelling at the collection. Afterwards, stroll the adjacent park or pop across to **BrewDog Glasgow** (p139) for a well-deserved pint.

EVENING

The Finnieston (p138) is great for a seafood dinner, or you might prefer a curry at **Mother India** (p135). Later, bop to the bands at legendary **King Tut's Wah Wah Hut** (p50).

A Short Break

MORNING

Investigate the fine **Hunterian Art Gallery** (p126), the gorgeous interiors of the **Mackintosh House** (p126) and the diverse collection of the **Hunterian Museum** (p124), all part of the **University of Glasgow** (p133).

AFTERNOON

Roam **Byres Rd**, checking out vintage shops and quality delicatessens. Take a lengthy stroll in the **Botanic Gardens** (pictured; p132) and check out pretty **Kelvingrove Park** (p134), dropping by **Inn Deep** (p140) for a waterside drink.

EVENING

Dine at the celebrated **Ubiquitous Chip** (p132) then see what's going down at **Òran Mór** (p138), a pub-cum-theatre set in a converted church. Alternatively, catch a gig at **The Stand** (p136) comedy club.

If You Have More Time

See what's on in the city during your stay, paying particular attention to what's coming up at the **OVO Hydro** (p113) and **SEC Armadillo** (p113) for big-name concerts and comedy; **Glasgow Film Theatre** (p48) and the **Centre for Contemporary Arts** (p50) for arthouse and experimental cinema; **Platform** (p52), **Classic Grand** (p52) and **Cathouse Rock Club** (p52) for live-music gigs; and **Hampden Park** (p111) and **Celtic Park** (p68) for football.

Follow a visit to the **Riverside Museum** (p102) or **Glasgow Science Centre** (p104) with a **powerboat trip** (p110) along the river Clyde, or pick up a public hire bike and ride the Clyde Walkway to **Cuningar Loop** (p112) and try your hand at bouldering. If time allows, consider a day trip on the historic paddle steamer **PS Waverley** (p112).

If architecture and design are your thing, spend a day in the Southside visiting both **House for an Art Lover** (p106) and **Holmwood House** (p110).

SEC Armadillo and OVO Hydro (p113)

KENSOFTTH/SHUTTERSTOCK ©

A City Day Trip

Glasgow has so much to see and do that many visitors return for a second or third time.

Morning Take a guided tour exploring the hidden corners of **Central Station** (pictuerd), then walk the city centre streets to appreciate their grand **Victorian architecture** (p42) before a street-food lunch at **Platform** (p52).

Afternoon Continue your architectural explorations on the streets of the **Merchant City** (p71), taking time to discover the **Gallery of Modern Art** (p81) and the **Glasgow Police Museum** (p86).

Evening Down a cocktail in **Artà** (p91) or **Corinthian Club** (p91), followed by a delicious dinner at the **Spanish Butcher** (p90).

On a Rainy Day

Glasgow is the rainiest city in the UK, with an average of 170 wet days each year – so be prepared. Fortunately it has many indoor attractions where you can stay dry.

You can easily spend half a day in either **Kelvingrove Art Gallery & Museum** (pictured; p120) or the **Burrell Collection** (p98). In the West End, the **Hunterian Museum** (p124), the **Hunterian Art Gallery** (p126) and **Mackintosh House** (p126) are just across the street from each other, and could also occupy another half a day.

Alternatively, go shopping in the dry, in arcades and malls such as **Argyll Arcade** (p92), **Princes Square** (p92), **Buchanan Galleries** (p53) and **St Enoch Centre** (p92).

Get Prepared

BOOK AHEAD

Three months before
Book for big-name concerts at the **OVO Hydro** (p113) and top restaurants such as **Ubiquitous Chip** (p132), **Glaschu** (p90) and **Ox & Finch** (p138).

One month before
Reserve a table for weekend seatings at popular restaurants and book tickets for major football matches.

One week before
This is usually enough notice to secure a table at most restaurants and to buy match tickets.

Manners Matter

Generally friendly, often with a cheeky, sarcastic sense of humour, Glasgow folk are more likely to offend than be offended. Conversations about football (particularly Celtic v Rangers) or Scottish independence might get heated. Local taxi drivers will launch into sweary, passionate rants if asked about Glasgow's Low Emission Zone. Best to play it safe and talk about the weather. It's customary to queue; don't skip ahead.

The Right Clothes

Glasgow comedian Billy Connolly famously said 'there's no such thing as bad weather, just the wrong clothes'. In Scotland, the whole 'four seasons in one day' saying is often true, so packing a little bit of everything is a wise approach. A waterproof jacket is a must; failure to bring one will inevitably result in torrential rain. Bring a comfy hat for cold, windy days.

Things to Know

Buying your round at the pub Like the rest of the UK, Glaswegians generally take it in turns to buy a round of drinks for the whole group, and everyone is expected to take part. The next round should always be bought before the previous round is finished. In pubs, you are expected to pay for drinks when you order them.

Language The Scots speak English with an accent that varies in strength – in Glasgow it can sometimes be unintelligible. If you're having trouble following someone's conversation, just ask them to slow down.

Accommodation Rates shoot up at weekends and can reach stratospheric levels, even at mediocre places, if there's a big-name concert on a Saturday night.

TIPPING

Tipping isn't usually expected in Glasgow and is reserved for good service in top-end hotels and restaurants.

Hotels
£1 per bag

Pubs & Bars
not expected

Restaurants
for good service

Taxis
round up to the
nearest pound

DAILY BUDGET

Budget: Less than £50

- Dorm bed: £15–35
- Museum admission: mostly free
- All-day bus ticket: £5.60
- Takeaway fish and chips: £8–12

Midrange: £50–150

- Double room at a midrange B&B: £65–110
- Pub lunch: £15
- Dinner at a midrange restaurant: £30–40
- Live gig: £3–10

Top End: More than £150

- Double room at a high-end hotel: £130–250
- Champagne afternoon tea: £50
- Dinner at a top restaurant: £60–80
- Big-name concert at the OVO Hydro: from £75

Currency
Pound sterling (£)

Language
English

Time zone
GMT/UTC

TIP

Public toilets are a bit thin on the ground; museums and galleries are your best bet, and the website *toiletmap.org.uk* is a great resource. Most are free; some have a small charge.

When To Go

It's up to you. Glasgow is a year-round destination where there is always something interesting to see and do.

Let's be honest, people don't visit Glasgow for the climate. Summer obviously has the better weather and the long daylight hours (the sun doesn't set until 10pm); allow extra time to explore. But spring and autumn often have more dry days, and in May you've got the colourful splash of cherry blossom on Glasgow Green, and in October the gold and russet of autumn leaves in Pollok Country Park. Winter is predictably cold and dark, but that just makes a warm pub and a whisky all the more appealing.

The Big Events

January: Glasgow doesn't have a huge New Year event like Edinburgh; the biggest gathering is the **Ashton Lane Hogmanay Street Party** in the West End. The cultural year kicks off with **Celtic Connections** (p89), a two-week celebration of folk, roots and world music exploring Scotland's connections with other cultures around the world with more than 300 shows spread across the city.

February/March: The cold, dark days of winter are livened up with the arrival of the **Glasgow Film Festival** (p48), one of the UK's top celebrations of cinema, with two weeks of world premieres, special events and guest Q&As. The fun continues with the **Glasgow International Comedy Festival** (p136), with 18 days of big-name acts and dozens of smaller gigs filling up the rest of March.

June: Held in even-numbered years, **Glasgow International** is an arts festival featuring a range of innovative installations, performances and exhibitions. In the West End, **WestFest** (p135) sees

Glasgow

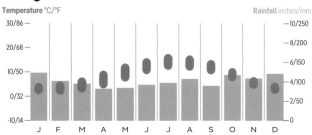

National Youth Pipe Band of Scotland at Celtic Connections (p89)

music, theatre, comedy and visual art events across the entire month of June.

July: For three action-packed days, **TRNSMT** festival draws major indie rock acts to Glasgow Green.

Pure Glasgow

May: The football season runs from August through to the following May, when the **Scottish Cup Final** is played at Hampden Park.

July/August: There's a lineup of famous names for 12 nights of live music at **Summer Nights at the Bandstand** in Kelvingrove Park.

August: More than 6000 pipers and 35,000 spectators descend on Glasgow Green for two days of the **World Pipe Band Championships** (p66), the biggest such competition on the planet.

December: The run-up to Christmas is **pantomime season**, which Glasgow enthusiastically embraces; the **Pavilion Theatre** (p46) is famed for its annual panto.

--- **ACCOMMODATION LOWDOWN** ---

Glasgow has plenty of accommodation but can still fill up at weekends; booking ahead is essential then, as well as in high season (July and August), and if there's a festival or big-name concert at the OVO Hydro.

Getting There

Most visitors arrive at Glasgow Airport (GLA), eight miles west of the city centre, or by rail at Glasgow Central Station.

From the Airport to the City Centre

By Bus

Glasgow Airport Express Bus 500 Every 10 to 15 minutes from 6.30am to midnight, and half-hourly or hourly through the night, from Stance No 1 outside the main Glasgow Airport terminal building, to Buchanan Bus Station via Central and Queen Street train stations (one way/open return £10.50/17, 25 minutes journey time). Buy a ticket from the driver, or using the FirstBus app. A FirstDay ticket (£16) gives unlimited bus travel on the day of purchase until 1am the following day, including the airport service.

First Bus No 77 Departs from Stance No 6 outside the main Glasgow Airport terminal every 60 minutes from around 8.30am to 10pm, and passes along Dumbarton Rd and Argyle St, which is more useful if you're heading to Partick or the West End.

By Taxi

The official white airport taxis can be picked up at the rank outside the main terminal building; no prebooking is needed. It takes around 15 minutes to get to the city centre and costs about £17 depending on the time of day and traffic.

Other Points of Entry

Glasgow Prestwick Airport (PIK)

Glasgow Prestwick Airport, 30 miles southwest of the city, is used by Ryanair and some other budget airlines. There's a train station at the airport, with four trains an hour (two on Sundays) to Glasgow (£10.40, 40 to 55 minutes). You get a 50% discount from the airport by showing your boarding pass. A taxi to the centre of Glasgow costs £70 to £80.

Train Stations

Trains from London Euston arrive at Glasgow Central Station, trains from Edinburgh arrive at Queen Street Station – both are in the city centre.

Getting Around

It's possible to get around Central Glasgow, the Merchant City and the East End on foot without sacrificing too much shoe leather, but for the West End and Southside you'll want to use bike, bus or subway. Bus is the main means of transport in the city; the subway only has one circular line.

Bus

Bus services, mostly run by First Glasgow, are frequent and cover most of the city, running from around 6am to midnight.

Limited night buses run hourly between midnight and 5am on Friday and Saturday nights only. You can buy tickets from the driver when you board, or via the First Bus app.

There are also City Sightseeing hop-on-hop-off buses (pictured right) with stops at all the major attractions in the centre, West End and Southside, and audio guides in multiple languages. They are more expensive than city buses, but are often more convenient for travel between the main tourist sights.

Subway

Glasgow's delightfully retro subway has only 15 stops along a circular route; there are two lines: outer

circle (clockwise, orange on maps and signs) and inner circle (anticlockwise, grey on maps and signs). Make sure you pick the right side of the platform.

The subway doesn't cover a large area, but it's the most convenient way of getting between the city centre and West End. Trains run every four minutes at peak times and

FROM LEFT: GARRY CORNES/ALAMY STOCK PHOTO ©, JEFF WHYTE/SHUTTERSTOCK ©

─── **ESSENTIAL APP** ───
Download the First Bus app for journey planning, mobile tickets and live bus times.

every six-to-eight minutes during off-peak, from 6.30am to 11.30pm Monday to Saturday, but only from 10am to 6pm on Sunday.

Bike

The NextBike public hire scheme is increasingly popular in the city. There are 800 bikes in circulation across 80 locations; cyclists can pick up and drop off at any of them. Download the NextBike app to use the system, and look for the pink People Make Glasgow branding on the bikes. Note that you can rent two at one time using a single account. Cycling isn't recommended for getting around the city in general, but is ideal for exploring sights along the Clyde Walkway, which runs on the north side of the river.

Train

There's an extensive suburban network of trains in and around Glasgow, run by the national carrier, ScotRail. The Cathcart Circle Line is especially useful for travel between Central Station and the Southside. Tickets can be purchased from ticket offices or by using the ScotRail app.

Taxi

There's no shortage of taxis, and if you want to know anything about Glasgow, striking up a conversation with a cabbie is a good place to start. Fares are reasonable – you can get from the city centre to the West End for around £6.

Public Transport Essentials

Bus Tickets

First Bus (*firstglasgow.com*) operates most of Glasgow's city bus services. You can buy a ticket from the driver when you board using cash (exact change only), a contactless card or mobile device, or use mobile tickets purchased via the First Bus app.

There's also a tap-on-tap-off digital payment system. You can travel on city buses by tapping on and off at the digital readers on the bus with your contactless credit card, debit card or mobile device.

You will only be charged the single fare for the journey you make (£2 within City Zone 1), but if you make additional journeys throughout the day, your payments will be capped at the cost of a day ticket (£5.60). If you travel on three days within a seven-day period, your payments will be capped at £15.50.

Subway Tickets

The Glasgow Subway is operated by Strathclyde Passenger Transport (*spt.co.uk*) and uses paper tickets (unless you are a resident, in which case you can buy a Smartcard which works across the subway, bus and rail).

You can buy tickets from machines at the entrance to all subway stations using your contactless credit card, debit card or mobile device, either a single journey ticket (£1.80) or a day ticket (£4.30).

Combined Tickets

You can buy a combined subway and City Sightseeing bus ticket that allows unlimited travel on both on the day of purchase (adult/child £21.80/11.50). Buy online at *citysightseeingglasgow.co.uk/get-tickets*. There are various Smartcard, ZoneCard and Glasgow Tripper tickets, but these are really only of use to residents and long-term visitors.

TRAVEL COSTS

Minimum adult bus fare
£2.00

Bus day ticket
£5.60

Minimum adult subway fare
£1.80

TRAVEL TIP

A combined one-day subway and City Sightseeing bus ticket offers good value and convenience.

TICKETS
Tickets can be purchased online (using the First Bus and ScotRail apps), from ticket machines in subway and train stations, and from ticket offices at train stations.

	Single trip	Day ticket
Bus	£2	£5.60
Subway	£1.80	£4.30
Suburban rail	£3.20	£7.40 (including subway)

TICKET ZONES

First Bus operates three fare zones, but City Zone 1 covers everything in this guidebook apart from Holmwood House (Zone 2).

🎁 A Few Surprises

One of Glasgow's big attractions is its many hidden quirks and curiosities that only reveal themselves to those who look closely.

The Gorbals

The Gorbals district lies just across the river from the Merchant City and the East End. It used to be one of the poorest parts of the city, an area of tenement slums blighted by poverty until the entire area was demolished in the 1960s and '70s. Cross **Gorbals St Bridge** today and you'll find modern offices and apartment buildings, but turn left on Cleland St to see a little-known memorial to three of the most famous people to come out of the Gorbals. The arches under the railway bridge hold beautiful **mural paintings** of artist **Hannah Frank** (1908–2008), boxing world champion **Benny Lynch** (1913–46) and **Allan Pinkerton** (1819–84) who emigrated to the USA, became Chicago's first police detective and founded the Pinkerton National Detective Agency.

The Clockwork Orange

Anyone who's familiar with the underground railway systems in London, Paris or New York is in for a surprise when they head down to the **Glasgow Subway**. It's so small. Not only is there only one circular line (it takes just 24 minutes to make a complete circuit), if you're over 6ft tall you'll have to duck to enter a carriage. In a dig at its toy-like size and corporate colours, Glaswegians have nicknamed it the Clockwork Orange.

Homeless Jesus

Outside St George's Tron Church, off Buchanan St, is a bronze figure of a homeless man sleeping on a bench. Look closely and you'll see the stigmata on his feet – the figure represents **Jesus Christ**, a reminder of the many people who live rough on Glasgow's streets.

OFFBEAT GLASGOW

Learn about Britain's oldest city police force and chat with retired officers at the **Glasgow Police Museum** (p86).

Look around the **Britannia Panopticon** (p88), the world's oldest surviving music hall, where Stan Laurel first trod the boards.

Poke your nose into secret tunnels and abandoned platforms on a **guided tour of Central Station** (p46).

Discover Glasgow's enormous contribution to medical science at the **Friends of Glasgow Royal Infirmary Museum** (p67).

PHOTO_./SHUTTERSTOCK ©

St Enoch station, Glasgow Subway (p37)

JEFF J MITCHELL/GETTY IMAGES ©

Britannia Panopticon (p88)

Explore Glasgow

Central Glasgow 37
East End 55
Merchant City 71
Southside & the Clyde 95
West End 117

Glasgow's Walking Tours
Central Glasgow 42
Art School Life 44
East End 62
A Stroll to the Barras 64
Merchant City 82
Shop the Style Mile 84
The Clyde 108
West End 128
Scale Woodland's Hill's Heights 130

Barrowland Ballroom (p65)
GEORGECLERK/GETTY IMAGES ©

See p51
for eating,
drinking and
shopping
listings

Explore
Central Glasgow

Stepping out of Central Station you are immediately immersed in the bustle and swirl of a metropolis. Crowds throng the pavements, intent on getting to offices or shops, and the streets are loud with honking traffic, queueing buses and impatient taxis, while an eclectic mix of modern and Victorian architecture looms above your head. Welcome to the centre of Scotland's biggest city. Central Glasgow changes character from east to west, going from a frenetic blend of transport terminals, pubs and shopping malls to the more sedate terraces of thoroughfares like Bath St, where upmarket offices sit over basements converted into stylish bars.

Getting around

 Bus
Glasgow's main Buchanan St Bus Station is located in the city centre, and numerous bus routes traverse the neighbourhood.

Ⓢ Subway
Buchanan St and St Enoch stations are in the centre of this neighbourhood, while Cowcaddens Station is in the north, handy for getting to and from the West End.

Ⓣ Train
Both of Glasgow's major train stations, Central and Queen Street, are in this area. Cathcart Circle trains from Glasgow Central link to the Southside.

★
THE BEST

GUIDED TOUR Glasgow Central Tours (p46)

VICTORIAN PUB The Horse Shoe Bar (p48)

CINEMA Glasgow Film Theatre (p48)

LIVE MUSIC King Tut's Wah Wah Hut (p50)

ARCHITECTURE AND DESIGN Mackintosh at the Willow (p40)

The Lighthouse (p46)
PAIKONG/SHUTTERSTOCK ©

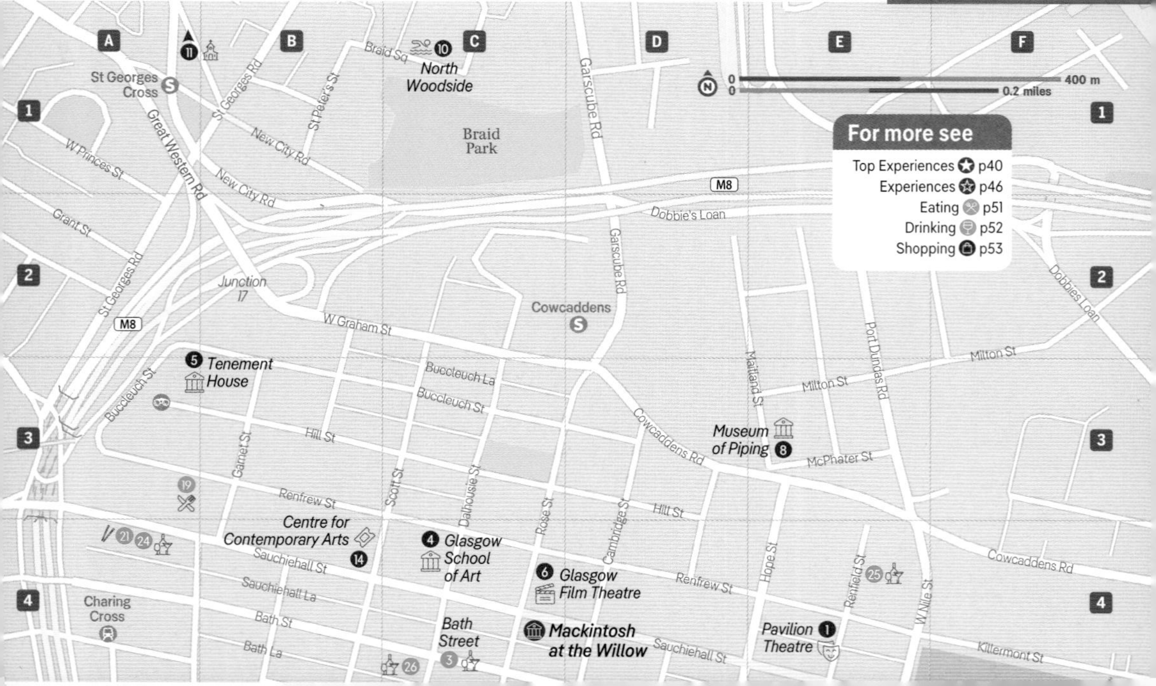

A
B
C
D
E
F
1
2
3
4
St Georges Cross
North Woodside
Braid Park
Braid Sq
Garscube Rd
St Georges Rd
St Peter's St
New City Rd
W Princes St
Great Western Rd
Grant St
M8
Dobbie's Loan
Dobbies Loan
Junction 17
Cowcaddens
W Graham St
Buccleuch La
Buccleuch St
Hill St
Garnet St
Scott St
Dalhousie St
Rose St
Cambridge St
Renfrew St
Sauchiehall St
Sauchiehall La
Bath St
Bath La
Charing Cross
Cowcaddens Rd
Maitland St
Milton St
Port Dundas Rd
McPhater St
Hope St
Renfield St
W Nile St
Killermont St
5 Tenement House
4 Glasgow School of Art
6 Glasgow Film Theatre
Mackintosh at the Willow
Centre for Contemporary Arts 14
Museum of Piping 8
Pavilion Theatre 1
Bath Street 3
10
11
19
21
24
25
26
0 400 m
0 0.2 miles
For more see
Top Experiences p40
Experiences p46
Eating p51
Drinking p52
Shopping p53

Queen St

George Sq

Dundas St

Cathedral St

Buchanan St

Saltmarket St

W Nile St

Buchanan St

Sauchiehall St

W Nile St

Renfield St

Bath St

Bath La

W Regent St

W George St

St Vincent St

Gordon St

Mitchell La

Buchanan St

Mitchell St

Argyle St

Queen St

Ingram St

Miller St

Argyle St

Argyle St

St Enoch Centre

St Enoch
St Enoch Sq

Howard St

Jamaica St

The Lighthouse

Union St

Drury St

Renfield La

Stereo

The Horse Shoe Bar

W George St

W Regent St

Hope St

Gordon St

Gordon St

Hope St

Central Station

New World

Oswald St

Midland St

Wellington St

Wellington La

W Campbell St

St Vincent La

Blythswood Sq

Blythswood St

W Regent St

W George St

Douglas St

St Vincent St

Bath La

St Vincent La

Bothwell St

Bothwell La

Waterloo St

Cadogan St

W Campbell La

Holm St

Argyle St

York St

James Watt St

Broomielaw

King Tut's
Wah Wah Hut

Holland St

Elmbank St

Pitt St

Pitt St

St Vincent St

Bothwell St

Bishop La

Anderston

Argyle St

Washington St

McAphine St

Clelea St

Carrick St

Brown St

Crimea St

India St

Newton St

North St

St Vincent St

M8

M8

Cheapside St

39

Mackintosh at the Willow

Mackintosh at the Willow is a faithful reconstruction of the original Willow Tea Rooms, designed and furnished by Charles Rennie Mackintosh in 1903 for restaurateur Kate Cranston. Here you can admire the architect's distinctive touch in just about every detail.

MAP P38, **C4**

PLANNING TIP
Book your tour tickets online and time your visit so that you can have lunch in the tearoom or, if the weather smiles, on the rooftop terrace.

Scan for practical information.

Exterior

Before you go in, step across Sauchiehall St and view the exterior. When Glasgow City Council gave permission for Ms Cranston to create a new tearoom, it was understood that the exterior would remain unchanged. Mackintosh ignored this requirement and created a curved, whitewashed frontage that displays his signature blend of Art Nouveau and Japanese influences, strikingly different from the traditional sandstone tenements on either side. It was very controversial at the time.

Ground Floor

Although the tearoom is open to the public, it's worth booking a 45-minute guided tour of the building as you'll get access to the upstairs rooms that are usually reserved for private events. The **front saloon** is a bright space, with a colour scheme of white, pale pink and green, suggestive of spring. Stylised willow-leaf motifs grace the gesso panels on the wall, and are repeated on the stairs and the balcony rail. The **back saloon** is darker and more intimate, with stencilled roses, lattice patterns and tall rectangular panels reminiscent of Japanese *shoji* sliding doors. Everywhere are Mackintosh's signature ladder-back chairs.

First Floor

Upstairs you'll be shown the glittering showpiece of the building, the **Salon de Luxe**, originally

STOCKEUROPE/ALAMY STOCK PHOTO ©

designed as a private room where ladies who lunch could entertain their guests. It's a spectacular space in white and silver, grey and purple, filled with reflected light from stained glass, Art-Nouveau mirrors and crystal chandeliers – like being inside a jewellery box with the Mackintosh levels turned up to 11. Next door is the **billiard room**, once the exclusive preserve of gentlemen. The room is modelled on a country house with dark wood panelling, but Mackintosh details abound.

Exhibition

After the tour, spend an hour exploring the two-level interactive exhibition about the Willow Tea Rooms' historical context and Cranston's long-lasting collaboration with Mackintosh and his wife, Margaret Macdonald.

QUICK BREAK
The obvious place for a break is the tearoom itself, but if you really want to spoil yourself, book a champagne afternoon tea in the Salon de Luxe.

🚶 **WALKING TOUR**

Walk Central Glasgow

Poet John Betjeman called Glasgow 'the greatest Victorian city in the world'. Its 19th-century heyday as a centre of international trade, shipbuilding and heavy engineering made it one of Britain's wealthiest cities. This walk explores that legacy, reflected in the grand Victorian architecture of Central Glasgow.

START	END	LENGTH
Glasgow Central Station	Hill St Viewpoint	1 mile; one hour

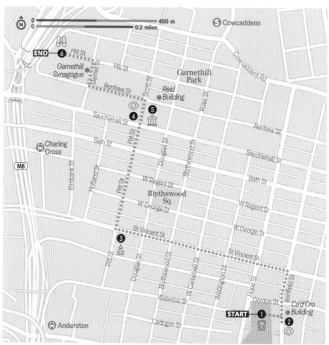

❶ The City's Beating Heart

Glasgow Central Station, opened in 1879, is Scotland's busiest train station and one of the finest Victorian railway terminuses in the world. The glass roof is a marvel of engineering, spanning an area of 4000 sq metres without any supporting pillars. Take the Union St exit (downstairs to the left as you're facing the departure information boards).

❷ Meet Alexander 'Greek' Thomson

Stepping out of Central Station you are presebted with busy Union St. Across the street rise the **Egyptian Halls** (1872), one of Alexander 'Greek' Thomson's A-listed Victorian masterpieces, laced with ancient Greek and Egyptian motifs. To its left are the stunning Venetian glass-and-iron arches of the Ca'd'Oro Building (1872).

❸ Neoclassical Splendour

Head west along St Vincent St, one of the city's best-preserved Victorian streets. It's lined with impressively ornate sandstone buildings, starting with the imposing Neoclassical facade of the Bank of Scotland, and ending at the unmistakable Greek temple of **St Vincent Street Church** (1859), the building that gave 'Greek' Thomson his nickname; its tower is a distinctive feature of the Glasgow skyline.

❹ Victorian Meets Contemporary

Follow Pitt St north to yet another Thomson creation, the Grecian Chambers (1865), now housing the **Centre for Contemporary Arts**. Note the classic Thomson features of symmetry, repetition and decorative Greek columns.

❺ Mackintosh Masterpiece

Continue north up the steep hill of Scott St to the plastic-swathed scaffolding that hides Charles Rennie Mackintosh's fire-damaged **Glasgow School of Art** (1897–1909); there are plans to restore it. Across the street is the GSA's ultramodern Reid Building (2014).

❻ West End Panorama

Go north on Garnet St and west on Hill St past Garnethill Synagogue (1879–81), Glasgow's oldest purpose-built synagogue. Hill St is the highest point in central Glasgow; there's an Insta-worthy panorama of West End spires from the **viewpoint** at its end.

🚶 **WALKING TOUR**

Art School Life

Mackintosh's famous Glasgow School of Art building may be down and damaged, but art college life goes on. Around the School are numerous bohemian hang-outs where students and the city's artier souls congregate. If you can't enrol in the School, at least you can spend an afternoon pretending that you have.

START	END	LENGTH
Singl-end	Nice N Sleazy	¾ mile; two to three hours

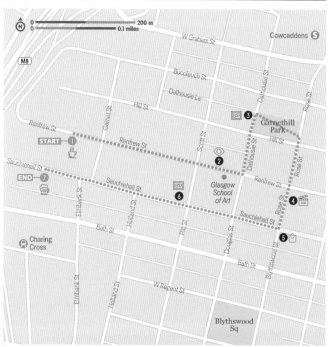

1 Get Caffeinated

There's something really life-enhancing about the atmosphere at basement cafe **Singl-end** (p51). Drop in here for an excellent cup of coffee, a vegan brunch or yummy home-baked cakes. Everything is delicious.

2 Graduate Art Shows

The School of Art's modernistic **Reid Building**, designed by Steven Holl, opened in 2014. Its crisp glassy shell contrasted totally with Mackintosh's red sandstone, but eerily matches the plastic wrapping on the scaffolding currently around his fire-damaged masterpiece. Check for graduate art shows in the Reid Building's gallery.

3 Air Your Laundry

The laundrette is a staple of student life, and the **Art Laundrette** is right around the corner from the School of Art. You may not need any clothes washed, but this laundrette hosts exhibitions, workshops and occasional live performances; poke your nose in to see if anything's on before sauntering through leafy Garnethill Park.

4 Going to the Pictures

No self-respecting art student would be seen dead in a main-stream cinema, so it's just as well that the arthouse (and Art Deco) **Glasgow Film Theatre** (p48) is close at hand. Opened in 1939 and then known as the Cosmo, it was the UK's first purpose-built arthouse cinema outside London.

5 Browse Some Vinyl

And no self-respecting art student would be without a record collection. Pop into **Assai Records** to admire the album art on their huge array of vinyl, and check for in-store events and live performances.

6 Contemporary Art

The **Centre for Contemporary Arts** (p50) is just that. It's a hive of creativity – drop by to see what's going on and to check out the visual art exhibition spaces. There are lots of shows and activities here too.

7 Sleazy Does It

There's a string of bars on this end of Sauchiehall St and they get pretty lively later in the evening with students lured by cheap lager. **Nice N Sleazy** (p52) is one of the best, where drinkers enjoy the wide beer selection, downstairs gigs and late opening.

EXPERIENCES

A Night at the Theatre

ENTERTAINMENT

MAP: **1** P38 E4

Glasgow's **Pavilion Theatre** (trafalgartickets.com) opened in 1904, one of the city's many variety theatres that began replacing the bawdier music halls from the 1890s on. It was built in French Renaissance style by the same architect who was responsible for London's Piccadilly Theatre and Manchester's Palace Theatre; the opulent interior was a feast of Rococo plasterwork, mahogany panelling and marble mosaic flooring.

Much of the theatre's Edwardian splendour survives to this day, making a night at the Pav a memorable experience. The programme includes big-name stand-up comics, tribute bands and nostalgia tours, but the biggest event is the annual **Christmas pantomime** (pavilionpanto.com), which runs from the beginning of December until mid-January.

Inside (& Under) Central Station

GUIDED TOUR

Dating from 1879 to 1905, Glasgow's Central Station is the bustling heart of Scotland's railway system, the terminus of lines from London Euston, Edinburgh and Inverness, and the hub of the city's suburban network. Join a one-hour walking tour with **Glasgow Central Tours** (glasgowcentral tours.co.uk; per person £15), and a passionate, entertaining guide will lead you around, behind and under the sprawling complex. Hidden vaults, an abandoned Victorian platform and intriguing information make this a fascinating experience even if railways in general don't get you excited.

Climb to the Top of the Lighthouse

ARCHITECTURE

MAP: **2** P38 E7

Charles Rennie Mackintosh's first public commission as an architect, completed in 1895, was a striking new headquarters for the Glasgow Herald newspaper. Tucked up a narrow lane off Buchanan St, The Lighthouse now serves as Scotland's **Centre for Architecture and Design** as well as the **Mackintosh Interpretation Centre**, a detailed (if slightly dry) overview of his life and work.

The most notable feature of the exterior is the octagonal tower that gives the building its name, which once housed a water tank and a doocot (Scots for dovecot) for homing pigeons, which were used to send horse-racing results to the paper in the early days. Inside, a magnificent spiral staircase, installed in 1999, lets you climb to the top floor of the 'lighthouse' for great views over the rooftops.

At the time of research the building remained closed to the public – check its Facebook page for reopening announcements.

Bar-Hopping on Bath Street

PUB CRAWL

MAP: **3** P38 **C4**

Begin at the legendary Horse Shoe Bar (p48), which dates from the late 19th century and is largely unchanged. It's a picturesque spot, with one of the longest continuous bars in the UK. Head up West Nile St for two blocks to the Shilling Brewing Co (p52), a brewpub housed in a grand former bank building; the citrussy Session IPA is a real palate cleanser. It's two blocks west and one north to the The Pot Still (p52), which has a time-warp feel with its creaky floor and wrought-iron tables, plus a superb whisky selection. Bath St is well-known for its selection of offbeat bars, including the Butterfly and the Pig (p53) with its shabby-chic decor, cosy retro feel and regular live jazz. A little further west is Bunker, another classic Bath St bar; both are open until 3am on Friday and Saturday.

Domestic History at the Tenement House

MUSEUM

MAP: **5** P38 **A3**

The tenement is a distinctive feature of Glasgow's streetscape, with long rows of bay windows and pointy turrets in distinctive red or beige sandstone. A tenement is a communal building, generally four storeys high, that is divided into flats (apartments) opening from a common stair. They were built mainly from 1850 to 1900 to house

GLASGOW SCHOOL OF ART

In 1896, aged 27, Charles Rennie Mackintosh won a competition for his design for a new building to house the **Glasgow School of Art**, where he had studied. This was his supreme architectural achievement, completed in 1909. Tragically, it was just about to reopen after a devastating 2014 fire when, unbelievably, another blaze in 2018 destroyed the painstakingly reconstructed interiors and severely damaged the building. The city has committed to reconstructing it, but it's unlikely to be completed before 2027.

MAP: **4** P38 **C4**

the huge increase in the city's population following the Industrial Revolution.

The Tenement House (*nts.org. uk; adult/child £8.50/6*) at 145 Buccleuch St was the home of Ms Agnes Toward from 1911 to 1965. When she died the new owner realised they had stumbled on a remarkable time capsule – the furniture and fittings all dated from the turn of the century – and rather than modernise it, they passed it on to the National Trust for Scotland who maintain it as a fantastic example of a typical early-20th-century middle-class Glasgow home complete with

MACKINTOSH QUEEN'S CROSS

Lying a mile north of the city centre, **Mackintosh Queen's Cross** (mackintoshchurch.com; adult/child £5/free) was the only one of Charles Rennie Mackintosh's church designs to be built, completed in 1899. You could easily walk past without noticing, but the window detail and the quirky tower give the game away. Inside, the architect's typically dark-hued woodwork is beautifully set off by deep blue and purple stained-glass windows and exquisite relief carvings; it's now headquarters of the Charles Rennie Mackintosh Society. Take bus 17, 60 or 61 from Hope St to the Bonawe St stop on Maryhill Rd.

MAP: 11 P38 A1

original furniture, kitchen range and gas lighting. There's even a pot of homemade jam dated 1929.

Movie Night   CINEMA

MAP: 6 P38 C4

Going to see a film, or – to use the correct Glaswegian term – going to the pictures, has been a hugely popular pastime here since the first cinemas opened in Edwardian times. By the 1930s, Glasgow had around 130 movie theatres, more per head of population than any other city outside the USA. Today there are mainstream cinemas everywhere, but true cinephiles will gravitate towards the **Glasgow Film Theatre** (glasgowfilm.org).

It first opened in 1939 as the Cosmo – the building is a gem of Art Deco design – and now has three screens presenting a diverse programme, ranging from the latest independent and international films to experimental features and big-screen classics. It also hosts the annual two-week **Glasgow Film Festival** in late February/early March; the festival celebrated its 20th anniversary in 2024.

Down a Pint in a Classic Victorian Pub   VICTORIAN PUB

MAP: 7 P38 E6

Hidden away on Drury St, **The Horse Shoe Bar** (thehorseshoebarglasgow.co.uk) has been a Glasgow institution for more than a century. It opened in 1884, one of three pubs owned by John Scouler, then the city's best known publican, who had a thing about horses. The other two, called The Snaffle Bit and The Spur, have since been demolished, but Scouler's creation lives on. It's a gleaming, mahogany-and-mirror-lined shrine to the pub's namesake motif, with horseshoe shapes everywhere from the fireplace to the vast island bar itself – at 32m it was the longest continuous bar in the UK until 2016 when it was pipped by the Bowland Beer Hall in Lancashire. Pop in for a pint, or stay for lunch

– once famous for its Scotch pies, the menu now extends to classic pub grub such as steak pie, fish and chips, burgers and pizzas.

Have a Blow at the Bagpipes
PIPING MUSEUM

MAP: **8** P38 E3

Glasgow's Museum of Piping (*thepipingcentre.co.uk; per person £5*), part of the National Piping Centre, covers the history of the Highland bagpipes. Several fine historic pieces, including pipes dating from the 18th century, are on display, plus instruments from Europe's other piping countries, such as Polish, Hungarian, Spanish and Italian bagpipes. It's worth timing your visit to catch the Meet the Piper guided tour (included in the admission fee; check the website for times); your guide will be an experienced bagpiper, and you will get a chance to play the chanter – the part of the pipes that plays the melody – yourself.

Going Underground
BAR

MAP: **9** P38 D8

Where Argyle St passes beneath the railway tracks of Central Station, an inconspicuous doorway leads into an underground wonderland of red-brick arches, built around 1905 to support the station above. Today, the first of six interconnected vaults is occupied by Platform (p52; *platformgla.co.uk*), a popular lounge bar and street food kitchen; the second by pool tables, shuffleboard and foosball; and the remainder reserved for live music and DJs, club nights and private events.

The subterranean venue was home to the legendary **Arches**, the godfather of Glaswegian clubs, from 1991 to 2015, pulling in the biggest names in dance music. It was revived in 2023 as New World (*newworldglasgow.com*) with a dozen or so club nights hosted in the original venue, spread across October, November and December,, the entrance is from the tunnel on Midland St, a block south of Argyle St.

Take a Dip in a Victorian Pool
SWIMMING POOL

MAP: **10** P38 C1

North Woodside (*glasgowclub .org/venues/north-woodside; adult/ child £4/2*) is the oldest surviving public swimming pool in Glasgow, opened in 1882. It originally had twenty-seven private baths for men, seven for women, and sixty-seven washing stalls in the 'steamie' (laundry). Around 60,000 people a year used the facility, charging a penny for adults and a half-penny for children. On Fridays a long queue would form as people waited for their weekly hot bath.

The swimming pool has been restored and is still open to the public, so you can enjoy a dip among the Victorian ceramic tiles, rows of cast-iron columns and ornate glazed roof, with changing cubicles ranged along the sides. You'll need to register (free) as a Pay As You Go member (*glasgow-club.org*), then book a session on their website. Note that the baths are closed at weekends.

See an Up-And-Coming Band at King Tut's
LIVE MUSIC

Glasgow is the king of Scotland's live music scene. Year after year, touring musicians and travellers alike name the city as one of their favourite places in the world to enjoy live music. There are lots of venues in the city centre, many with free gigs almost every night, including bars like MacSorley's (p53), **Stereo** (MAP: ⑫ P38 D6) and Nice N Sleazy (p52).

But the city's premier spot is **King Tut's Wah Wah Hut** (MAP: ⑬ P38 B5; *kingtuts.co.uk*), hosting bands every night of the week. King Tut's has been a mainstay of the Scottish live music scene since 1990 – the list of big-name artists who kicked off their careers here would fill a book, and includes Radiohead, Pulp, My Chemical Romance, Florence & The Machine, Biffy Clyro, Manic Street Preachers, Frightened Rabbit and Paolo Nutini; Oasis were famously signed to their first record label at the venue in 1993.

Today the line-up features the best of new music from across the UK and further afield, with the occasional blast of nostalgia from the likes of Tom Robinson, Snow Patrol and The Killers.

Explore Avant-Garde Arts
ARTS VENUE

MAP: ⑭ P38 **B4**

Glasgow's **Centre for Contemporary Arts** began life in 1974 as the Third Eye Centre, founded by playwright Tom McGrath. It was an arts space that rapidly became the epicentre of Glasgow's counter culture: Edwin Morgan, Allen Ginsberg, Billy Connolly, Whoopi Goldberg and John Byrne all performed here, and it played host to early exhibitions of the works of artists such as Peter Howson, Ken Currie and Damien Hirst.

It was succeeded in 1992 by the Centre for Contemporary Arts (*cca-glasgow.com*), a nonprofit that hosts exhibitions, events, films, music, literature, plays, workshops, festivals and performance art, still housed in the same distinctive building – Alexander 'Greek' Thomson's Grecian Chambers on Sauchiehall St.

The gallery space puts on several major exhibitions of contemporary art each year (closed Sunday and Monday) – past exhibitors have included Tracey Moffatt, Marvin Gaye Chetwynd and Rachel Maclean – while the performance areas have a packed schedule of avant-garde events; check the website for what's on.

Best Places for...

€ Budget €€ Midrange €€€ Top End

Eating

See p38 for map of locations

Scottish

Red Onion €€
15 C5

This comfortable split-level bistro buzzes with contented chatter. French, Mediterranean and Asian touches add intrigue to classic Scottish cookery. *red-onion. co.uk; noon-9pm Mon-Sat, to 7.30pm Sun*

Gamba €€€
16 C5

In a business-district basement is one of the city's premier seafood restaurants. Presentation is elegant, with carefully selected flavours allowing the fish, sustainably sourced from Scotland and beyond, to shine. *gamba.co.uk; noon-2pm & 5-9pm Wed-Fri, noon-9pm Sat*

Cafes

Riverhill Coffee Bar €
17 E6

Chain cafes plaster Glasgow's centre, so it's a joy to come across this tiny place, which offers great coffee and hot chocolate. *riverhillcoffee. co.uk; 8am-4pm Mon-Fri, from 9am Sat*

Willow Tea Rooms €€
18 E7

A recreation of the tearooms designed by Charles Rennie Mackintosh in 1904 with good teas and bagels, pastries or, more splendidly, champagne afternoon tea. *willowtearooms. co.uk; 9am-6pm*

Singl-end €€
19 A3

This basement cafe covers a lot of bases, with good coffee, generous breakfasts and lunches, booze and baking. Dietary requirements are superbly catered for. *thesingl-end.co.uk; 9am-5pm*

Laboratorio Espresso €
20 E5

The best coffee we've tried in Glasgow, sourced properly and served in delicious double-shot creations with authentically concentrated espresso. There are a couple of tables outside, and it also serves paninis and Italian desserts. *laboratorioespresso.com; 8am-5.30pm Mon-Fri, from 9am Sat, from 10.30am Sun*

Asian

Loon Fung €€
21 A4

An elegant Cantonese oasis that's one of Scotland's most authentic Chinese restaurants. The dim-sum choices are toothsome, and the seafood is really excellent. *loonfungglasgow. com; noon-11pm*

Bar Soba €€
22 E7

Both the bar and downstairs restaurant do quality Asian fusion. Background beats are

51

also perfect for chilling with a cocktail. *barsoba. co.uk; noon-10pm*

Drinking

Bars

Platform
23 D8

Lively, family-friendly and dog-friendly, these atmospheric brick-arched vaults beneath the railway lines house a cocktail bar and street food kitchen. *platformgla. co.uk; 4-11pm Thu, noon-midnight Fri & Sat, noon-9pm Sun*

Nice N Sleazy
24 A4

On the rowdy Sauchiehall strip, students from the nearby School of Art make the atmosphere here reliably friendly. If you're over 35, you'll feel like a professor not a punter. *nicensleazy.com; 5pm-3am Fri & Sat*

Flying Duck
25 E4

Venture down the graffiti-splashed stairs to this bohemian cellar space, where there's a sociable studenty vibe, vegan comfort food and regular bands or club

nights. *theflyingduck.org; 9pm-1am Fri & Sat*

Slouch Bar
26 C4

There's a basement bar for all types on Bath St, with a range of vibes. This one is low-lit and casual but handsomely designed, with an American South feel to the decor, drinks and rock soundtrack. *slouch-bar. co.uk; 4pm-3am Sun-Thu, from noon Fri & Sat*

Clubs

Sub Club
27 D8

Scotland's most famous house club, still going strong several decades on. Saturdays here are one of Glasgow's legendary nights out, offering serious clubbing with a sound system that aficionados rate as the city's best. *subclub.co.uk; typically 11pm-4am Thu, Fri & Sat*

Buff Club
28 C5

Tucked away in a lane behind the Bath St bar strip, this club presents eclectic, honest music without pretensions. The sounds can range from hip-hop to disco via electronica. *thebuffclub. com; 11pm-3am Mon, Tue & Thu-Sat*

Classic Grand
29 D8

Rock, industrial, electronic and powerpop grace the stage and the turntables at this unpretentious central venue with cheap drinks and welcoming locals. *classicgrand.com; hours vary*

Cathouse Rock Club
30 D8

It's mostly rock, alternative and metal with some Goth and post-punk at this long-standing indie spot with two dance floors. Upstairs is intense; down-stairs is more tranquil. *cathouse.co.uk; 11pm-3am Wed-Sun, to 4am Sat*

Pubs

The Pot Still
31 D5

This charming and comfortable spot has a nostlagic atmosphere with period furnishings. It boasts an exellent selection of whisky. *thepotstill. co.uk; 11am-midnight*

Shilling Brewing Co
32 E6

Former bank building that's now a microbrewery with huge windows and room to try its own and guest beers. *shillingbrew ingcompany.co.uk; noon-11pm Mon, to midnight Tue-Thu, to 1am Fri & Sat, 12.30-11pm Sun*

MacSorley's

 D8

There's nothing better than a good horse-shoe-shaped Glasgow bar like this. Its elegantly moulded windows and ceiling add a touch of class. This happy place also offers live music nightly. *macsorleys.co.uk; 11am-midnight Tue-Sun*

Butterfly and the Pig

 C5

A breath of fresh air, this offbeat basement spot makes you feel comfortable as soon as you plunge in. There's a wonderful tearoom upstairs, great for breakfast before the pub opens. *thebutterfly andthepig.com; noon-late*

Waterloo Bar

 C7

Traditional Waterloo Bar is Scotland's oldest gay pub. It attracts punters of all ages, is very friendly and, with a large group of regulars, a good place to meet people away from the scene. *facebook.com/ waterloobar1; noon-11pm Sun-Thu, to midnight Fri & Sat*

The Horse Shoe Bar

 E6

This legendary pub and popular meeting place dates from the late 19th century and remains

largely unchanged. It's a picturesque spot, but its main attraction are real ale and good cheer. *thehorseshoebarglasgow. co.uk; 11am-midnight*

Drum & Monkey

 E6

Dark wood and marble columns frame this attractive drinking emporium, peppered with church pews and leather lounge chairs. There's tank beer and several real ales on tap. *nicholsonspubs.co.uk; noon-11.30pm Sun-Thu, to midnight Fri & Sat*

Shopping

Music

Love Music

 F6

An independent record shop that stocks a good selection of vinyl and has regular in-store performances. Strongest on rock, alternative and punk, with lots of Scottish bands featured. *lovemusicglasgow.com; 11.15am-5pm Mon-Sat*

Clothing

Slanj Kilts

 E8

This upbeat shop is a top spot to hire or buy

kilts, both traditional and modern, as well as other tartan wear, a range of T-shirts and other accessories. *slanjkilts.com; 9.30am-5.30pm Mon-Sat, 11am-4pm Sun*

Adventure 1

 F5

This friendly, no-frills outdoor shop is an excellent place to buy outdoor clothing, hiking boots, backpacks and military surplus gear. *adventure1. co.uk; 9am-5.30pm Mon-Fri, 9.30am-5pm Sat*

Celtic Store

 E8

Your one-stop shop for all green-and-white footballing gear and Celtic memorabilia. There's a larger shop at Celtic's stadium and one at the airport. *celticfc. com; 9am-6pm Mon-Sat, 11am-5pm Sun*

Shopping Malls

Buchanan Galleries

 F5

At the junction of Sauchiehall and Buchanan Sts, this shopping mall has a huge number of contemporary clothing retailers as well as a John Lewis department store. *buchanangalleries.co.uk; 9am-6pm Mon-Wed, Fri & Sat, to 7pm Thu, 10am-6pm Sun*

See p69
for eating
and drinking
listings

Explore
East End

The East End is where medieval Glasgow grew up, stretching along the High St from the cathedral district south to the river. Today it's home to the oldest surviving buildings in the city, including Glasgow Cathedral and Provand's Lordship, and also to former Victorian slum districts that were demolished in the 1930s and replaced with tenements and tower blocks – areas such as Calton and Bridgeton that are fast regenerating as hubs of creative activity. Calton, once famous for its linen mills, remains one of Britain's poorest districts but hums with life at its famous weekend Barras market.

Getting around

 On Foot

It's a 15-minute walk from George Sq to the cathedral, or 20 minutes to the Barras market; from the cathedral to the Barras is also a 20-minute walk.

 Bus

Public transport is not very helpful for getting around the East End, and walking is often faster. To get from the city centre to the People's Palace, take bus 18 from Union St opposite Central Station to the Green St stop on London Rd.

★
THE BEST

GOTHIC ARCHITECTURE
Glasgow Cathedral (p57)

FLEA MARKET The Barras
(p66)

BREWERY TOUR Tennent's
Brewery (p67)

CITY PARK Glasgow Green
(p66)

MUSEUM St Mungo Museum
of Religious Life & Art (p60)

McLennan Arch, Glasgow Green (p66)
KENSOFTTH/SHUTTERSTOCK ©

N
0 ——————— 200 m
0 ——————— 0.1 miles

For more see

Top Experiences ⭐ p57
Experiences ⭐ p66
Eating ✖ p69
Drinking 🍺 p69

Stirling Rd

Castle St

Cathedral St

Taylor St

Collins St

Rottenrow East

Cathedral Sq

High St

George St

Montrose St

Ingram St

Merchant Square

Albion St

Blackfriars St

High St

Bell St

MERCHANT CITY

Trongate

Glasgow Cross

High St

St Andrew's St

London Rd

Gallowgate

Greendyke St

London Rd

McLennan Arch ❸

Glasgow Green

Nelson's Monument ⚓ ❷

People's Palace

River Clyde

Friends of Glasgow Royal Infirmary Museum 🏛 ❻

Glasgow Cathedral ⛪

St Mungo Museum of Religious Life & Art 🏛

Provand's Lordship 🏛 ❹

🗡 ⑫ ⑪ 🗡

Glasgow Necropolis 🏛

Cathedral St

Wishart St

DENNISTOUN 🍺 ⑬

Duke St

Tennent's Brewery 🍺 ❺

Duke St

🍺 ⑮

🗡 ⑩

the Barras 🏛 ❶

Moncur St

Stevenson St W

London Rd

Gilbert St

🗡 ⑧

CALTON

Gallowgate

Barrack St

Maitland St

Montieth Row

Binnie Pl

🍺 ⑭

London Pl

🗡 ❼

🗡 ⑨

Glasgow Cathedral

Glasgow Cathedral has a rare timelessness. The dark, imposing interior conjures up medieval might and sends a shiver down your spine. It's a shining example of Gothic architecture and, unlike nearly all of Scotland's other cathedrals, it survived the turmoil of the Reformation almost intact.

MAP P56, **D1**

History

Glasgow grew up around the Gothic cathedral that was built upon the tomb of St Mungo between 1250 and 1500; an even older cathedral occupied the site from 1136. Unlike other religious buildings in Scotland, it came through the Protestant Reformation of 1560 (when many Catholic churches were defaced or destroyed) with little damage. Except for the cathedral, which is the oldest surviving structure in Glasgow, virtually nothing of the medieval city remains.

Nave

As you walk into the nave, the first thing you'll notice is its great height – 32m – and slender grace. The wooden roof has been restored many times since its original construction, but some of the timber dates from the 14th century. Turn around and look back at the west window, Francis Spear's **The Creation** (1958), with Adam and Eve centre stage. The aisles, separated by elegant arcades, are flanked with tombs and war memorials hung with regimental colours, and the **old bell** of 1790, recast from its 16th-century predecessor.

PLANNING TIP
There are helpful volunteer guides throughout the cathedral; don't hesitate to speak to them as they can point out some interesting details. Although entry is free, donations are appreciated.

Scan for practical information.

The Creation (p57)

QUICK BREAK
Just across John Knox St from the cathedral is the family-friendly Italian restaurant **Celentano's**. A little further down the hill **Drygate** is a craft brewery that serves all-day food.

Eastern End

The quire, at the eastern end of the church, is divided from the nave by a late 15th-century stone quire screen, or **pulpitum**. It's decorated with seven characterful pairs of figures that may represent the seven deadly sins. Going through it, you are confronted with a splendid vista of the quire stalls leading to the four narrow lancets of the **east window**, another evocative work by Francis Spear depicting the Four Apostles.

The **upper chapter house** is in the northeast-ern corner, a mostly 15th-century space used as a sacristy; the University of Glasgow was founded here in 1451 before moving to its own premises. The **oak doors** here are the only original ones in the cathedral – note the bullet holes and lead shot embedded in the wood that testify to violent episodes in the 16th century.

Lower Church

The cathedral was built on a sloping site, meaning there is a lower level beneath the quire; not, strictly speaking, a crypt, as it is not below ground level. This vaulted lower church is an atmospheric space with a forest of thick columns – as you descend the south staircase, you can see a column from the older 12th-century cathedral. A modern altar stands over the supposed location of the **tomb of St Mungo**. This area was built in the mid-13th century to provide a more fitting setting for the saint's resting place.

Ambulatory

The sunken ambulatory at the eastern end has four square chapels separated by arches; this area featured as L'Hôpital des Anges in Paris in season two of *Outlander*. The **tomb of Bishop Wishart**, a key supporter of Robert the Bruce and an important figure in the cathedral's construction, is here. In the corner of the southernmost chapel is a **well** that was likely venerated before the cathedral was built and perhaps even before Christianity came to the area.

Blackadder Aisle

After the gloomy gravitas of the rest of the cathedral, the spectacular whitewashed vaulting of the Blackadder Aisle (also spelled Blacader) feels like a ray of sunshine. Commissioned by Robert Blackadder, Bishop of Glasgow from 1483 to 1508, it was originally designed as the crypt for a chapel to be built above, but this was never constructed. Look for the roof carving of a **laughing skull** with worms crawling out of the eye sockets.

ST MUNGO
St Mungo, who died in 603, is Glasgow's patron saint. His legend grew in the 11th and 12th centuries, and his tomb became a major medieval pilgrimage destination.

STEWART OF MINTO PLAQUE
About halfway along the south wall of the nave is one of the cathedral's oldest memorials, a worn brass plaque with the figure of a kneeling knight, dated 1606.

★ TOP EXPERIENCE

St Mungo Museum of Religious Life & Art

The St Mungo Museum of Religious Life & Art takes an impartial look at the six major world religions through the lens of art, from medieval times to modern. The overview of how faiths tackle the big questions of humanity – birth, marriage, death – is fascinating, and make this place a brilliant under-the-radar attraction.

MAP P56, **C1**

PLANNING TIP

The museum is popular with school groups, but you've got the cathedral and Provand's Lordship to see here too, so you can work your visit around these busy times.

Scan for practical information.

Gallery of Religious Art

Beautiful stained-glass saints and angels created by pre-Raphaelite **Edward Burne-Jones** gaze over this collection of religious art, including a statue of the Buddha, an Indigenous-Australian Dreaming painting and Native American totems. More stained glass from the 14th and 15th centuries stands alongside powerful modern paintings by war artists Robert McNeil and Peter Howson, notably **Massacre at Srebrenica** (2019).

Gallery of Religious Life

This gallery is the museum's heart, a compact but immersive space that presents how different cultures and religions approach major life events through photographs and objects. Birth, death, coming of age, sex, marriage, war, the afterlife; it's all here, with perspectives from Benin to British Columbia, from the Day of the Dead to bar mitzvahs.

Religion in Scotland

The top-floor exhibition covers religion in Scotland, including the Reformation, missionaries, sectarianism, multiculturalism and the increasingly secular Scottish society. A striking picture window looks out at Glasgow Cathedral and the Necropolis, with information on the bishop's palace that once stood here, and of which this building is a partial recreation.

Glasgow Necropolis

Behind Glasgow Cathedral, the vast 19th-century Glasgow Necropolis stretches picturesquely up and over a green hill, dotted with around 3500 gravestones. The elaborate Victorian tombs of the city's wealthy industrialists make for an intriguing stroll offering great views and a vague Gothic thrill.

MAP P56, **D2**

History

Once a Victorian pleasure garden called Fir Park, the hill behind the cathedral was converted to a cemetery in the 1830s and rapidly became popular with the city's upper classes. It is interdenominational – indeed, the first burial was a Jewish man in 1832 – and is a spectacular spot for a wander. There are more than 50,000 burials here and 3500 grand monuments, including some designed by Alexander Thomson and one by Charles Rennie Mackintosh.

Monuments

From the cathedral, the entrance to the Necropolis is via the **Bridge of Sighs** over the valley of the Molendinar Burn (now culverted), where St Mungo is said to have fished for salmon. Turn left and follow the zigzag path uphill, pausing to admire the ornate monuments. Styles range from Ancient Greek to Moorish to Baroque; most impressive of all is the **Monteath Mausoleum** (1850), like a circular Templar church with Hindu motifs (the deceased was an officer in the East India Company).

On the summit stands an 1825 monument to the Protestant reformer **John Knox**. The views back to the cathedral, with the Glasgow Royal Infirmary (1905) to its right, are stunning.

PLANNING TIP
You can buy a guidebook to the Necropolis online or in the shop at St Mungo Museum, or take a guided walking tour (see website for details).

Scan for practical information.

EXPLORE

EAST END

Walk the East End

The medieval city grew up along the High St, which links Glasgow Cathedral to the River Clyde and Glasgow Green. While little from this period remains, modern murals recall its history alongside others that celebrate more modern figures, while the Green itself continues to provide rest and relaxation.

START	END	LENGTH
Cathedral Square	People's Palace	2 miles; 1½ hours

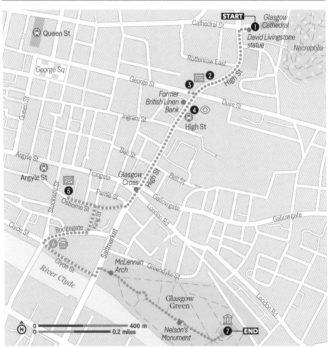

1 Cathedral Square

The square in front of Glasgow Cathedral has a statue depicting David Livingstone (1813–73), the Scottish-born doctor, missionary and explorer who was the first European to view Lake Nyasa and Victoria Falls in Africa.

2 Mungo Mural

As you head downhill along High St, a gable end is adorned with a giant mural painting of a bearded man in a bobble hat with a robin redbreast perched on his finger. This is a depiction of St Mungo, the patron saint of Glasgow. As a boy, he is said to have brought a robin back to life after some callous youths killed it – the first of his many miracles.

3 More Murals

At the junction with George St, detour a short distance to the right to find another mural of a woman and baby, depicting St Enoch, a sixth-century princess and the mother of St Mungo.

4 Old College

Continue down High St, a mishmash of modern buildings, open ground and a solitary Victorian relic – the former British Linen Bank with its elegant green cupola. Across the street, a train station occupies the former site of Old College, home of Glasgow University from 1460 until it moved to the West End in the 1870s.

5 The Big Yin

Although High St is the oldest street in the city, little of historical interest remains apart from the 17th-century Tolbooth Steeple at Glasgow Cross. Bear right into Osborne St to see the iconic mural of comedian Billy Connolly, based on the portrait by his friend, playwright John Byrne.

6 The Clutha & Charles Rennie Mackintosh

There are more murals at the Clutha and Victoria Bar, including one of Charles Rennie Mackintosh. Take a break at this 200-year-old venue for a drink or some food, then follow the riverbank east and through the McLennan Arch into Glasgow Green, a public park since 1450.

7 People's Palace

Stroll through the dear green space of the park, past the 44m-tall pillar of Nelson's Monument, raised in 1806, decades before Nelson's Column in London, to finish at the Victorian jewel of the People's Palace.

EXPLORE

EAST END

A Stroll to the Barras

The weekend Barras markets bring Glaswegians down to the East End in numbers. It's a traditional, working-class part of town, and the markets blend that heritage with a few rascals on the make, some glorious vintage shops and a posse of creatives doing design and street food. It's a great snapshot of the city.

START	END	LENGTH
Glasgow Cross	St Luke's & the Winged Ox	1 mile; one hour

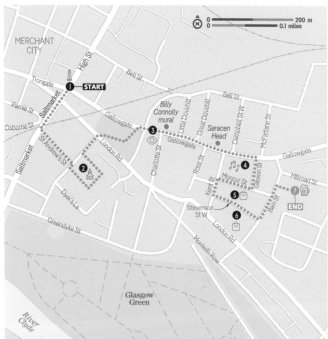

① Glasgow Cross

Start your stroll at Glasgow Cross. The Tolbooth Steeple dates from 1626, a clock tower that was once part of the old town hall; the pillar topped by a unicorn is the Mercat Cross, where royal decree mandated that a market could be held.

② St Andrews in the Square

Head south on Saltmarket to the handsome church of St Andrews in the Square, now home to a cultural centre. Built in 1756, it is one of the finest Neoclassical churches in Scotland, with its Corinthian columns, refined steeple and pediment carved with the city crest.

③ Road to the Barras

The Gallowgate is a typical East End mixture of Polish delis, kebab vendors and mobile-phone repair shops; the gable-end mural of Billy Connolly was one of three painted to mark the comedian's 75th birthday. Nearby is the Saracen Head (p69), known locally as the 'Sarry Heid', a classic East End pub favoured by Celtic football supporters.

④ All Kinds of Dancing

The Barrowland Ballroom is an old dance hall that is now one of Glasgow's most iconic music venues, with a second-hand market on the ground floor. Around the corner is a mural dedicated to the 2020 Booker Prize–winning novel *Shuggie Bain*, set in Glasgow's East End, by Scottish-American writer Douglas Stuart.

⑤ The New Barras

In the middle of the Barras area you'll find Barras Art & Design (p66), a modern counterpart to the traditional stalls showcasing the work of local artists. It's quite a contrast to the rest of the markets but it works very well.

⑥ Vintage Shopping

Disguised by a rather unremarkable facade, the paradise of the past that is Randall's Antique & Vintage Centre has some two-dozen vendors peddling an excellent range of vintage objects. Delving into times gone by makes for an addictive browse.

⑦ A Converted Church

End your stroll with a refreshing pint at St Luke's & the Winged Ox (p69), a pub set in a converted church.

EXPERIENCES

Spend a Saturday at the Barras

MARKET

MAP: ❶ P56 C4

Glasgow's legendary weekend flea market, the **Barras** (*barrowland. co.uk*), is a fascinating mixture of up-to-the-minute modernity and traditional working-class Glasgow, catering to a cosmopolitan mix of locals and visitors. Old stalls selling timefaded photographs, posters and DVDs that you'd struggle to give away are juxtaposed with vintage classics, sustainable fashion, earthy traders' pubs and a street scene where fake designer gear is marked down and dodgy characters peddle smuggled cigarettes.

Right in the heart of the Barras district, look out for **Barras Art & Design** (*baadglasgow.com*), which has given a fresh impetus to the market with its pop-up stalls, regular live music, busy courtyard bar and a menu of fusion food.

Take a Walk Around Glasgow Green

CITY PARK

Established by the Bishop of Glasgow in the mid-15th century, **Glasgow Green** (MAP: ❷ P56 B6) is the city's oldest public park, a venue for strollers, dog walkers and summer festivals. The main entry point is at the west end, through the imposing **McLennan Arch** (MAP: ❸ P56 A5). This 18th-century archway was originally the entrance to the Assembly Rooms on Ingram St, south of George Sq.

When that building was demolished, the arch was preserved and occupied several locations before ending up here in 1991.

The Green is home to several other monuments, notably the tall pillar of **Nelson's Monument** and a statue of James Watt (1736–1819), the Scottish inventor whose improvements to the steam engine ushered in the Industrial Revolution.

Visit the Oldest House in Glasgow

HISTORIC BUILDING

MAP: ❹ P56 C2

Across the street from the cathedral stands **Provand's Lordship** (*glasgowlife.org.uk; admission free*), the oldest house in Glasgow. This rare example of 15th-century domestic Scottish architecture was built in 1471 as a manse (a church minister's house). The ceilings and doorways are low, and the rooms are furnished with period furniture and artefacts. Upstairs a room recreates the living space of an early-16th century chaplain. There's also a fascinating exhibition of paintings of old Glasgow, showing how the city looked in the 18th and 19th centuries.

Thrill to the Skirl of the Pipes

MUSIC

Each summer Glasgow Green resounds to the sound of hundreds of bagpipes as the **World Pipe Band Championships** (*rspba.org*) get under way. Held on the third weekend of August, the competition draws more than 35,000 spectators to see bands from all over the world compete for the prestigious title.

The championships have been held annually since 1947, and Glasgow Green has been the venue since 1986. You can buy tickets in advance at the *glasgowlife.org.uk* website, or on the day at box offices at the entrances to Glasgow Green.

Take a Tour of Tennent's Brewery

MAP: ⑤ P56 **D3**

BREWERY

Despite these days of craft beers and boutique microbreweries, one in every three pints drunk in Scotland is still Tennent's lager – and that's a lot of pints. Tennent's was first brewed in 1885, and today more than two hundred million litres are produced yearly, commanding 60% of the Scottish lager market.

Tennent's Brewery (*tennents.co.uk; tours per person £20*) is the oldest continuously operating commercial location in Glasgow. It was founded on its current site, on the banks of the Molendinar Burn below the Necropolis hill, in 1740 by brothers Hugh and Robert Tennent (though an ancestor had brewed beer on the same site as long ago as 1556).

Fun, comprehensive 90-minute tours of the brewery run hourly from 11am to 4pm daily, except Monday. It's best to prebook by phone or online. No under-12s are allowed.

Marvel at Glasgow's Pioneering Medical History

MAP: ⑥ P56 **C1**

MUSEUM

The grand Neoclassical building rising to the north of Glasgow Cathedral is Glasgow Royal Infirmary. Established in 1794, it has often been at the forefront of medical science. The small **Friends of Glasgow Royal Infirmary Museum** (*friendsofgri.org; admission free; closed Sunday and Monday*) opened here in 2022, using old photographs, documents, notebooks and scientific instruments to tell the stories of some

 THE DEAR GREEN PLACE

The origins of Glasgow's name are lost in the mists of time, but probably come from the Brittonic or Gaelic words glas chu, meaning a grey-green hollow. This might refer to the valley of the Molendinar Burn, where St Mungo established a religious community in the 6th century on the site now occupied by the cathedral. 'Dear Green Place' as a popular nickname for Glasgow is based on the English translation of Glaschu, and was popularised by a short documentary film of the same name, released in 1968. Today 32% of the city is given over to green space, the second highest level in the UK after Edinburgh.

of Glasgow's pioneers of medical science. Joseph Lister revolutionised medicine by introducing antiseptic surgery in 1865, while John MacIntyre, an electrician turned doctor, developed the world's first radiology department here in 1896. The museum entrance is on Cathedral Square

Watch the Football at Paradise Park

FOOTBALL

MAP: **7** P56 **D6**

One of world football's most passionate and bitter rivalries divides Glasgow; when Celtic and Rangers, known as the Old Firm, take to the field, they aren't just disputing a league or a cup but, in part, playing out old divisions between Catholics and Protestants, Ireland and Britain, establishment and rebellion, and Celt and Anglo-Saxon.

Celtic FC, founded in 1887, plays in green and white hoops, and traditionally represents the Catholic side of the divide. They were the first British team to win the European Cup (in 1967) and are one of only five clubs in the world to have won more than 100 trophies.

Their home ground is Celtic Park (*celticfc.com*), also known as Parkhead or Paradise. Attending a match here guarantees a great atmosphere; tickets can be purchased on the club website. There are daily stadium tours (adult/child £17.50/12) where you visit the boardroom, dressing rooms, players' tunnel and dugout. To get here, take bus 2 or 61 from Ingram St to the Society St stop on Gallowgate, a 10-minute walk from the stadium.

 CELTIC VS RANGERS

The rivalry between Glasgow's two biggest football clubs is one of the oldest and most intense in sporting history, reflecting the sectarian tensions that have plagued Scotland and Ireland since the Battle of the Boyne in 1690. Although most supporters don't get involved with sectarianism, Rangers fans are still seen as mainly Protestant, and Celtic as mainly Catholic. The size and support of the two clubs has led to their dominance of Scottish football. They have won over 100 league championships between them and have met more than 440 times with a very even spread of results.

Best Places for...

❸ Budget   **❸❸** Midrange   **❸❸❸** Top End

Eating

Pub Grub

St Luke's & the Winged Ox **❸❸**

8 C5

This cosy pub (attached to a repurposed church that hosts live music every weekend) serves quality comfort food, from huge plates of nachos to burgers and fish and chips. *stlukes glasgow.com; noon-9pm*

Whistler on the Green **❸❸**

9 A5

On the northwest corner of Glasgow Green, this modern gastropub dishes up honest, wholesome pub grub; Sunday roast includes fish and vegetarian options. *whistleron-thegreen.co.uk; 5-9pm Mon, from noon Tue-Sat, noon-7pm Sun*

Van Winkle **❸❸**

10 C4

Handy for the Barras, this pub serves a classic American-style menu including burgers, Philly cheesesteak and French dip; there's a beer garden at the back. *vanwinkle. co.uk; noon-10pm*

Italian

Celentano's **❸❸❸**

11 C2

Set in the gorgeous Cathedral House Hotel, built in 1896 in Scottish Baronial style, this is a family-friendly, Italian-inspired restaurant offering seasonal sharing menus. *celentanosglasgow.com; noon-3pm & 6-10pm Wed-Sat, noon-6pm Sun*

Cafes

Copperbox Coffee **❸**

12 C2

Beautifully set in an old 'Tardis' police box, this tiny outlet will serve you a soul-restoring cup of coffee and make a tasty sandwich to order. Perfect for a quick break while sightseeing in the area. *instagram.com/ copperboxcoffee; 10am-3pm Sun-Fri, to 4pm Sat*

See p56 for map of locations

Drinking

Pubs

Drygate

13 D2

Craft brewery where you can watch the beer being made as you sip one of two dozen on tap in the convivial, industrially fitted interior, or sit out on the terrace. *drygate.com; 11am-midnight*

West on the Green

14 D6

This spacious brewpub is housed in an ornate former carpet factory. It brews beers to the traditional German purity laws. *westbeer.com; 11am-11pm Sun-Thu, to midnight Fri & Sat*

Saracen Head

15 C4

A classic East End pub, known to the locals as 'the Sarry Heid', that dates from 1904. A favoured haunt of Celtic supporters, it's packed on match days. *noon-midnight*

69

See p90
for eating,
drinking and
shopping
listings

Explore
Merchant City

What was once the domain of the Victorian industrialists, whose palaces of trade and commerce dignify the area, the Merchant City is now a playground of restaurants, bars and shops. Just strolling around is the best way to get to grips with the neighbourhood, which is better appreciated as an architectural ensemble than as a list of must-see attractions. Remember to look up at the facades of the buildings you are passing; many were trade guilds, mercantile exchanges, shipping company offices or organs of state, with elegant Neoclassical facades and quirky architectural details.

Getting around

🚶 On Foot
The Merchant City is a compact neighbour-hood, barely half a mile square; you can walk across it in any direction in about 10 minutes.

Ⓢ Subway
St Enoch subway station in the southwest corner of the district is handy for getting to and from the West End.

★

THE BEST

HISTORIC BUILDING
City Chambers(p74)

MUSEUM Glasgow Police
Museum (p86)

ART GALLERY Gallery of
Modern Art (p81)

GUIDED TOURS Glasgow
Music City Tours (p89)

AFTERNOON TEA
Corinthian Club (p86)

Duke of Wellington, Gallery of Modern Art (p86)
MEUNIERD/SHUTTERSTOCK ©

A B C D

1

St Vincent St

St Vincent Pl

W Nile St

Buchanan St

Buchanan St

George Sq

Queen St

S Frederick St

**George
Square**

**City
Chambers**

George Sq

Cochrane St

N Court La 🍴 15

Gordon St

Royal Exchange Sq

Exchange Pl

2

Mitchell La

**Gallery of
Modern Art**

Ingram St

Hanover St

S Frederick St

Ingram St

*Corinthian
Club* 2

19 🍴

14 🍴

Virginia Pl

Virginia St

29

Glassford St

17

Springfield Ct

33 🛍

Buchanan St

Queen St

Miller St

24 🎭

30

31

Virginia Ct

39 🛍

Wilson St

3

52 🛍

18 🍴

Argyle St

4

St Enoch
S

St Enoch
Sq

Argyle St

Dunlop St

Virginia St

Glassford St

Hutcheson St

Trongate

Osborne St

🅿
**Argyle
St**

Stockwell St

5

34 🛍

Howard St

**Billy
Connolly** 8

Old Wynd

Osborne St

6

Clyde St

Maxwell St

Dunlop St

Stockwell Pl

Stockwell St

Howard St

River Clyde A B C D

E
F
G
H

1

John St
Montrose St
Richmond St
N Portland St

George St

George St
7

2

Cochrane St
John St
Montrose St
Ramshorn Graveyard
Albion St
Shuttle St
Cottage St

Ingram St
13 Fellow Glasgow Residents
9
Ingram St

Hutcheson St
Brunswick St
Garth St
21
16 **3** City Halls
20 Old **4** Fruitmarket
5 Merchant Square Market
Albion St
Blackfriars St
22
High St

3

Wilson St
12
10 **25**
Walls St

MERCHANT CITY
Bell St
Glasgow Police Museum **1** **23**
Bell St

4

Candleriggs
Albion St
Tontine La
High St
Bell St

Trongate
Sharmanka Kinetic Theatre
Britannia **6** Panopticon
36
37
Trongate

5

New Wynd
King St
Parnie St
Chisholm St
38
High St

Osborne St

6

King St
11
35
Osborne St

For more see

Top Experiences ⭐ p74
Experiences ⭐ p86
Eating ✗ p90
Drinking 🍺 p91
Shopping 🛍 p92

N
0   200 m
0   0.1 miles

E
F
G
H

City Chambers

Glasgow's town hall, City Chambers, is one of Scotland's most impressive buildings. It was built in the 1880s in a Beaux-Arts-inspired blend of Neoclassical and Venetian-style architecture, and was opened by Queen Victoria in 1888 after going five times over budget.

MAP P72, **D1**

PLANNING TIP

Free 45-minute guided tours run from Monday to Friday at 10.30am and 2.30pm. You can't book in advance; turn up 20 minutes ahead of time to ensure a place.

Scan for practical information.

Exterior

The building's imposing four-storey main facade made a powerful statement about Glasgow's wealth when it was erected, and it is still impressive today. It incorporates both Neoclassical and Neo-baroque elements and is backed by a soaring bell tower. Elegant Venetian windows run along the higher floors, flanked on the top level by sculptures representing the worthy ideals of the age.

The triangular pediment above the entrance shows Queen Victoria on her throne, receiving the gifts of Scotland, England, Ireland and Empire. Look at the top of the pediment to see '**Scotland's Statue of Liberty**', representing Truth holding a flaming torch aloft, bordered by the figures of Riches and Honour.

Foyer

The foyer, free to visit during opening hours, is an impressive space, with polished red-granite columns, caryatids glistening with mica and elaborate mosaic work on the floor and ceiling – a real artisanal labour recalling Glasgow's former preeminence as a port city. Based on the miracles

AGF SRL/ALAMY STOCK PHOTO ©

attributed to St Mungo, Glasgow's patron saint, the city's distinctive crest appears on the floor just inside the entrance, with the motto '**Let Glasgow Flourish**' (pictured). The main symbols are a tree (oak), bird (robin), fish (salmon) and bell, immortalised in a mnemonic learned by all Glasgow schoolchildren – Here is the tree that never grew / Here is the bird that never flew / Here is the fish that never swam / Here is the bell that never rang – and in the 1989 pop song 'Mother Glasgow' by local band Hue & Cry. Note that the fish has a gold ring in its mouth – legend has it that a jealous king threw the ring into the Clyde and then demanded his queen produce it on pain of death. St Mungo sent a monk to fish in the river, who brought back a salmon, and Mungo retrieved the ring from its mouth, thus sparing the queen's life.

QUICK BREAK
Paesano Pizza, a block and a half south of George Square, is a good lunch spot; a little further on is **Brutti Compadres**, a congenial tapas bar.

Staircases

To go beyond the foyer, you need to take a guided tour. The interiors, designed in ornate Italian Renaissance style, are even more impressive than the outside and have been used as film sets to represent the Kremlin and the Vatican. The twin three-level staircases in various Carrara marbles and alabaster are the largest in Western Europe, a majestic feature reminiscent of an MC Escher engraving, and one of the reasons why the building cost so much – some of the panels had to be painted to look like marble to get the project over the line. As you climb the stairs, rub the lion's nose for luck, as generations of council staff have done before you.

Debating Chamber

The city council only meets here every six weeks, so tours can usually enter the chamber. It's a stunning room decked out in hand-carved Spanish mahogany. You can sit in the councillors' very comfortable red-leather seats arranged in a semicircle before the Lord Provost's throne. In front of that is a holder for the ceremonial mace, while at either end of the chamber are ornate fireplaces topped by the city crest.

Banqueting Hall

The banqueting hall is a magnificent space more than 15m high. The carpet design mirrors the pattern of the gilded and coffered ceiling; the brass chandeliers are best appreciated from the minstrel's gallery above. Murals and paintings by several of the **Glasgow Boys** line the hall, with depictions of arts and crafts; the virtues; the rivers Tay, Forth, Clyde and Tweed; and images of St Mungo, shipbuilding and the Glasgow fair.

Picture Gallery

The top floor is lined with a series of portraits of former Lord Provosts and other Glasgow worthies under a glass cupola. It's interesting to see the varied styles at work as different artists, at different times, took on their subjects. Check out Peter Howson's cheekily irreverent **portrait of Pat Lally**, a Labour politician and provost from 1995 to 1999, nicknamed Lazarus because of his numerous political comebacks.

HORNEL PAINTING
The **Satinwood Suite**, next to the Debating Chamber, features a painting by EA Hornel portraying springtime; all seven girls in the painting are modelled on one girl – the artist's niece.

★ TOP EXPERIENCE

Sharmanka Kinetic Theatre

Glasgow's most unusual sight is tucked away upstairs in an arts centre, but make sure you track Sharmanka Kinetic Theatre down to see a show. Meeting the bizarre and wondrous creations of Eduard Bersudsky, a sculptor and mechanic, is a real privilege for adults and children alike.

MAP P72, **E5**

PLANNING TIP
The weekly schedule features a variety of shows suitable for all ages. Arrive early and examine the sculptures before the show starts; the detail on them is impressive.

Scan for practical information.

Background

Bersudsky moved to Scotland in the 1990s from Russia, where he had already begun creating his 'kinemats'. These delightful and extraordinarily detailed mechanical sculptures crafted from scrap metal and elaborately carved wood, fitted with motors and – it seems – a soul, are set to music. Each one performs a story; these are sometimes humorous, sometimes deeply sad, but always acutely wry commentaries on the human condition. They often focus on Russian themes.

Self-Portrait with Monkey

With its lugubrious face, body of linked chains and horned head, this is one of the most poignant of Bersudsky's kinemats. Sharmanka means 'barrel organ' and this strange figure cranks a mangle (for wringing water out of washed clothes) and taps its booted feet, while a traditional Russian song of love and loss plays. A monkey swings from a pendulum between its legs. It's not hard to feel the artist's sense of sadness about his self-imposed exile from Russia.

Rag 'n' Bone Man

Bersudsky has often sourced his materials from the nearby Barras market (p64), and this curious (to say the least) figure is a tribute to the traders there. With fans for hands, a whir of cogs, sewing-

SHARMANKA KINETIC THEATRE/ROBIN MITCHELL ©

machine parts and typewriter keys for innards, a
wise wooden human-animal face with pince-nez,
a bell hanging from its nose and a strange figure
riding a stuffed bird atop its head, this is one of the
most delightful pieces in the collection.

Time of Rats

The sturdy wooden tunnelling machine at the
base is a mole with a long nose and a tail, and four
spiked wheels – it represents Russia, strong and
powerful but blind. The structure on its back is
covered with cavorting rats playing with various
contraptions: a typewriter, a gramophone, a sewing
machine. They represent those who control and
benefit from the artist's homeland; you can see why
Soviet politicians were not impressed by Bersudsky's art.

★ TOP EXPERIENCE

George Square

George Square is the city's biggest and grandest public square. It has traditionally been the gathering place for protests and demonstrations, notably a pro-Scottish independence rally in 2014. It has also been a set for films and TV shows, including *Succession* and *World War Z*.

MAP P72, **C1**

PLANNING TIP
The Glasgow Free Walking Tour (*freetourglasgow. com*) runs daily at 10.30am from the war memorial in George Square, starting with a tour round the square itself.

Scan this QR code for a live webcam view of the square.

History

Named after King George III, the square was laid out in 1781 but not fully built up until the late 19th century. It was famously the site of the **Battle of George Square** in 1919 when protesting workers clashed with police. Fearing a Bolshevik-style revolution, the government sent in 10,000 troops and six tanks to quell the riot.

Historic Buildings

The east side is occupied by the grand **City Chambers** (p74). Clockwise from here, on the south side, are the former **General Post Office** (1878), Chicago-style **Lomond House** (1924), and Neoclassical **Monteith House** (1863) and **Olympic House** (1905); and on the west side the former **Bank of Scotland** (1870) and the grand **Merchants' House** (1874) with its domed tower topped by a sailing ship on a globe.

Statues & Monuments

A dozen statues of famous figures grace the square, most prominently **Sir Walter Scott** atop the central column, and an equestrian statue of **Queen Victoria**. See if you can spot poet **Robert Burns**, engineer **James Watt** and police pioneer **Sir Robert Peel**. A pair of charismatic lions guard the war memorial.

★ **TOP EXPERIENCE**

Gallery of Modern Art

The Gallery of Modern Art features contemporary works from local and international artists, housed in a graceful Neoclassical building. The original interior is an ornate contrast to the inventive art often on display, though quality varies markedly by exhibition.

MAP P72, **B2**

The Building

The striking building that houses the gallery, with its handsome cupola and Greek temple frontage of Corinthian columns, was originally the **Royal Exchange** (1827) where merchants would meet to trade in cotton, linen, coal, iron and other commodities. It occupies the site of an even older building (1776), the private residence of tobacco lord William Cunninghame.

Stones Steeped in History

The elliptical balconies above the entrance hall host a permanent exhibition detailing the history of the building and its connections with the slave trade – Cunninghame owned plantations in the Caribbean and much of his, and Glasgow's, wealth was acquired through the trade in sugar and tobacco.

The Galleries

Galleries 1 and 3 are reserved for temporary exhibitions, while Gallery 2 focuses on recent acquisitions. Gallery 4 is the heart of the collection, titled **Domestic Bliss** in an ironic nod to the building's previous existence as a private home. Take a seat and watch the curator's video, then check out works by Grayson Perry, Mandy McIntosh and Anne Collier, and Alasdair Gray's **City Recorder** paintings documenting ordinary Glasgow lives.

PLANNING TIP
The basement of the gallery houses a cafe and a public library, a comfortable place to escape the city bustle for a while, or rest your legs after browsing the exhibits.

Scan for practical information.

☗ WALKING TOUR

Walk the Merchant City

This walk introduces the historic buildings of the Merchant City, dating from the 18th century when the transatlantic tobacco trade brought wealth flooding into Glasgow, and the 19th century when shipbuilding and textiles kept the industrialists prosperous.

START	END	LENGTH
George Square	Merchant Square	¾ mile; one hour

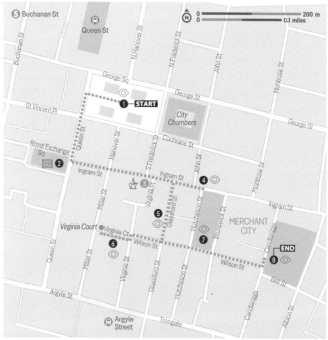

1 George Square

Stately George Sq is the civic centre of Glasgow, dominated by the City Chambers (p74) on the eastern side and dignified by statues of famous local folk.

2 Gallery of Modern Art

Walk one block south down Queen St to the Gallery of Modern Art. This striking colonnaded building, built in 1827, was once the Royal Exchange, a meeting place where merchants gathered to deal in commodities and services.

3 Corinthian Club

The Gallery of Modern Art faces Ingram St, which you should follow east to the Corinthian Club bar and casino, built in 1842 as a bank, and take a look at the breathtakingly extravagant plasterwork and soaring glass dome.

4 Hutcheson's Hall

Continue along Ingram St to Hutcheson's Hall – you'll see its distinctive slender spire on the left. It was built in 1805 as a hospital, replacing an earlier one founded by George and Thomas Hutcheson whose 17th-century statues grace the facade.

5 Trades Hall

Head south down Glassford St past Trades Hall, one of the Merchant City's most notable buildings, with its green dome. The sober Neoclassical facade was designed by Robert Adam in 1791 to house the trades guild and is the only surviving Adam building in Glasgow.

6 Tobacco Warehouses

Turn right into Wilson St and continue to Virginia St, which is lined with old tobacco warehouses. Many of these have been converted into cocktail bars, fashion boutiques and apartments – duck through the archway at Virginia Court, the former site of the Tobacco Exchange, for a look.

7 Old Sheriff Court

Head back along Wilson St to the huge six-columned portico of the Old Sheriff Court, built in 1844 in Ionic style. It was abandoned in 1986 and has since been developed as luxury apartments.

8 Merchant Square

Continue east on Wilson St to the colonnaded facade of Merchant Square, a covered courtyard that was built in the 1880s as part of the city's fruit market but now bustles with cafes and bars.

Shop the Style Mile

Glasgow's pedestrianised central streets are devoted to retail and people come from all over Scotland to shop here. Most of the stores are familiar chains, but having so many concentrated in one area is what pulls the crowds. The stretch from Argyle St to the north end of Buchanan St is known as the Style Mile.

START	END	LENGTH
Gallery of Modern Art	Buchanan Galleries	1½ miles / 1 hour

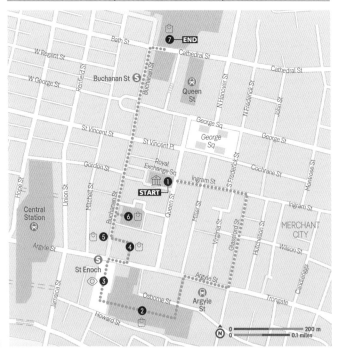

EXPLORE

MERCHANT CITY

WALKING TOUR

1 Ingram Street

Start your journey outside the Gallery of Modern Art (p81). The Duke of Wellington (with a traffic cone on his head) points the way down Ingram St, where you'll find several upmarket stores such as Ralph Lauren, Emporio Armani, Mulberry, Boss, Gant and Cruise.

2 St Enoch Centre

Head south to the pedestrianised section of Argyle St and the Dunlop St entrance to the glass-roofed palace of St Enoch shopping centre; it's good for families with Hamleys toys and Bunny & Bear clothing, but there are lots of high-street favourites too.

3 St Enoch Square

Exit at the far end into St Enoch Square. The quirky, turreted Victorian building (1896) was once the ticket office for the subway; it now houses a cafe.

4 All That Glitters

Opened in 1827, the beautiful Argyll Arcade (p92) connects Argyle and Buchanan Sts via a 90-degree turn. Take the time to chat with the cheerful, top-hatted doorpeople, then head into a glass-roofed arcade wholly devoted to jewellery and watch retailers.

5 Victorian Grandeur

Exit the far end and enter Frasers department store across the street. The heart of the building is a magnificent, five-level, glass-roofed atrium, a relic of the Victorian furniture store Wylie & Lochhead; you can still see 'W&L' carved in stone above the main entrance.

6 Peacock Palace

With all the finery on offer in the Style Mile, the unmissable peacock facade is an appropriate symbol for the gorgeously renovated historic shopping centre Princes Square (p92). Inside, it's all wrought iron and light, with a range of fashion stores including Kurt Geiger, Kate Spade New York and French Connection.

7 Top of the Hill

Weighed down by your numerous purchases, you stagger up Buchanan St, where it looks like the shops might finally come to an end. But no, here's Buchanan Galleries (p53), with John Lewis and more than 80 other retailers, including Schuh, Mango and Scottish Design Exchange.

EXPERIENCES

Instagram the Duke and the Traffic Cone
PHOTO OPPORTUNITY

If you want to sum up your trip to Glasgow in a single Instagram image, look no further than the equestrian statue in front of the Gallery of Modern Art in Royal Exchange Square. It's a statue of the Duke of Wellington – with a traffic cone on his head.

The story of the cone dates back to the 1980s, when it first appeared on the duke's head, probably the act of a student after a few beers. A decades-long struggle followed between the council (who kept removing it) and the citizens (who kept replacing it) – the citizens eventually won and so the cone survives as a symbol of Glasgow's sense of humour and its democratic will. It even gets dressed up for special events – rainbow colours for Glasgow Pride, gold during the 2014 Commonwealth Games and blue and yellow in support of Ukraine. It's a reminder that Glaswegians are deeply proud of their working class background and anti-establishment tradition.

Investigate the UK's oldest city police force
MUSEUM

MAP: **1** P72 **F4**

A little-known fact for pub quiz aficionados – the UK's oldest city police force is not London's Metropolitan Police (founded 1829), but the City of Glasgow Police (founded 1800). This is just one of many historical gems revealed by the **Glasgow Police Museum** (*policemuseum.org.uk; admission free*). Tucked away up a staircase opposite Merchant Square, this intriguing collection is worth an hour of anyone's time.

Among the uniforms, old photographs and records of notorious crimes, including the 1960s Bible John murders and the 1950 theft of the Stone of Destiny, are nuggets like the fact that Charles Rennie Mackintosh's father was a police superintendent, and secured the young architect's first paid commission: to design a gravestone for Chief Constable Alexander McCall who died in 1888 and is buried in the Necropolis.

If you can, get chatting to the retired officers who staff the place and are a fount of fascinating tales about the city.

Take Afternoon Tea at the Corinthian Club
EATING OUT

MAP: **2** P72 **D2**

The building at 191 Ingram St is one of the most ornate in a district that is not short of decorative architecture. Dating originally from the 18th century, it was rebuilt as a bank in 1841. Later, it was converted to offices, then to a sheriff's court, and finally to the Corinthian Club (*thecorinthianclub.co.uk*) in the late 20th century. The Ingram St facade is a wedding cake of Venetian-style extravagance, studded with statues and coats of arms.

But it's the interior that really takes the cake, thanks to Corinthian pilasters, coffered ceilings and elaborate plasterwork. Indulge yourself by booking a champagne afternoon tea in the palatial splendour of the club's **Teller's Bar**, with its soaring glass dome and ornate gilded cornices, where you can absorb the legacy of the era when Glasgow was a powerhouse of the British Empire.

Follow the Glasgow Mural Trail
STREET ART

Since 2008 Glasgow has been brightening up vacant sites and exposed gable ends in the city centre by encouraging the creation of mural paintings. In recent years more than 30 of these artworks have been gathered together in a **City Centre Mural Trail** (*citycentremuraltrail.co.uk*) that you can follow; there's an interactive map on the website, or download a pdf version of the map at *glasgow.gov. uk* (enter 'mural' in the search box).

The trail begins in the East End, where the most famous murals – of the city's patron saints, St Mungo and St Enoch – can be found just off the High St (p63), but most of the pieces are concentrated within the Merchant City and nearby.

Enjoy a Classical Music Concert at City Halls
LIVE MUSIC

The BBC Scottish Symphony Orchestra was Scotland's first full-time professional orchestra, established in 1935 by BBC Radio. Originally based at the BBC's Glasgow headquarters in the West End, it moved to the refurbished **City Halls** (MAP: ❸ P72 F3 ; *glasgowlife.org. uk*) in the Merchant City in 2006. The City Halls have been around since 1841 – the rectangular auditorium is known by performers from around the world as having superb acoustics – and stages weekly concerts by both the BBC SSO and the Scottish Chamber Orchestra.

Next door to City Halls is the **Old Fruitmarket** (MAP: ❹ P72 F3), a Victorian market hall that has been converted into an atmospheric performance space, complete with original cast-iron columns and vaulted roof. It also stages concerts ranging from folk and pop to jazz and world music.

You can browse the programme for both venues and buy tickets online on the GlasgowLife website.

Browse the Stalls at Merchant Square
MARKET

MAP: ❺ P72 **F4**

Merchant Square is a complex of bars, restaurants and entertainment venues housed in the city's former fruit and vegetable market. Every Saturday and Sunday from 11am to 5pm the central hall is given over to the Merchant Square Market (*merchantsquareglasgow. com*) with stalls peddling handmade arts and crafts, jewellery, homeware and baking, nearly all made locally in Glasgow.

Hop Aboard a City Sightseeing Bus

TOUR

The red, open-topped double-decker buses of **City Sightseeing Glasgow** (*citysightseeingglasgow. co.uk; adult/child from £18/10*) offer a choice of two routes, both starting on George Sq. The red route includes the Merchant City, Central Glasgow and the West End, while the yellow route concentrates on the East End and Southside. Buses depart every 15 minutes (every 30 minutes November to March) from 9am to 5.30pm and you can get on and off as you wish, making them a useful alternative to the city bus services and the subway.

Tickets can be bought online, and are valid for one or two days. All buses have wheelchair access and multilingual commentary.

Discover the World's Oldest Music Hall

MUSIC HALL

MAP: **6** P72 **E5**

Back in 1906, a 16-year-old Stan Laurel made his stage debut at Glasgow's **Britannia Panopticon** (*britanniapanopticon.org*) music hall before going on to fame and fortune as one half of the comedy duo Laurel and Hardy. The Britannia opened in 1857 and is the world's oldest surviving music hall. It closed down in 1938, but since 1997 an enthusiastic team of volunteers have been in the gradual process of restoring it – today it remains very much a work in progress, so be prepared for its somewhat down-at-heel appearance and lack of heating.

In support of the conservation project, the venue stages a range of shows from comedy to drag queens to pantomime, as well as the occasional Laurel and Hardy film night. If you can't make a show, the music hall is open to the public

---

 **TOBACCO LORDS**

The wealth that flowed into Glasgow in the 18th and 19th centuries from the tobacco, rum and sugar trades is reflected in the imposing Victorian architecture funded by the city's merchants and industrialists. The men who grew rich on the back of the transatlantic trade – and the evils of slavery that underpinned it – became known as the 'tobacco lords', and the Merchant City is filled with reminders of their legacy. In March 2022, Glasgow City Council publicly apologised for the city's part in the slave trade, saying the 'tentacles' of money from it reached every corner of the city.

---

to look around from noon to 5pm Thursday to Saturday (adult/child £2/1). The entrance is tucked away down the narrow alley of New Wynd, off Trongate.

Walk the City of Music   TOUR

In 2008, Glasgow became the world's third UNESCO City of Music in recognition of its legendary music scene. To learn more, join one of the guided walks run by **Glasgow Music City Tours** (*glasgowmusiccitytours.com; adult/child £19.50/14*); their Merchant City tour begins at the Clutha & Victoria Bar (p115) and takes in the Britannia Panopticon (p88), City Halls and Old Fruitmarket (p87) before heading to the Barrowland Ballroom (p65) in the East End. Prepare to be regaled with entertaining stories about the various venues, like the notorious 1977 Stranglers gig at City Halls which resulted in the city council banning punk rock concerts.

Tap Your Toes to Celtic Connections   MUSIC FESTIVAL

One of the advantages of a winter break in Glasgow is the opportunity to tune in to the **Celtic Connections** (*celticconnections.com*) festival. This celebration of folk, roots and world music explores Scottish music's links with other cultures around the globe, with 300 events spread across more than 30 locations all over the city, including City Halls and the Old Fruitmarket (p87) in the Merchant City.

The two-week festival takes place in the second half of January; a comprehensive events calendar and online ticket sales are available on the website.

BEST MERCHANT CITY MURALS

Glasgow's ongoing mural-painting project, begun in 2008, continues to enhance neglected spots around town. There are now more than 30 murals scattered across the city centre.

St Enoch & Child

MAP: **7** P72 **H2**

A modern take on Glasgow's founding story, with St Enoch cradling her child, St Mungo. The bird is a symbol of St Mungo.

Billy Connolly

MAP: **8** P72 **D5**

Based on a portrait by Connolly's friend, the artist and playwright John Byrne, painted to celebrate the comedian's 75th birthday.

Fellow Glasgow Residents

MAP: **9** P72 **F3**

Cleverly painted trompe l'oeil holes in the wall reveal all types of animals found in Glasgow's parks.

See p72 for map of locations

Best Places for...

€ Budget   **€€** Midrange   **€€€** Top End

Eating

Cafes

Café Gandolfi **€€**
 G4

Covers all the bases with excellent breakfasts and coffee, an enticing upstairs bar (p91) and top-notch bistro food in an atmospheric medieval-like setting. *cafe gandolfi.com; 8am-5pm Mon, to 10.30pm Tue-Sat, 9am-5pm Sun*

Mono **€**
11 F6

Combining vegan food and decent beer with a record shop (p93), ultra-casual Mono is a boho Glasgow classic. *mono cafebar.com; 11am-10pm Mon-Sat, from noon Sun*

Wilson Street Pantry **€€**
12 F4

This seriously cool cafe is brunch central – the inventive menu takes classic dishes and adds a twist, like eggs Benedict with Italian sausage instead of ham. *wilsonstreetpantry.com; 9am-4pm*

Spitfire Espresso **€**
13 F3

An appealing cafe close to Strathclyde University campus, Spitfire serves up superb coffees alongside a tempting breakfast and brunch menu. *spitfireespresso. com; 8am-5pm Sun-Thu, to 6pm Fri & Sat*

Fine Dining

Spanish Butcher **€€€**
14 C3

The moodily dark industrial decor above retro wickerwork chairs provides a fine setting for quality northern Spanish beef, with the best cuts designed for sharing. *spanishbutcher. com; noon-11pm Sun-Thu, 8am-midnight Fri & Sat*

Glaschu **€€€**
15 B2

A haven of fine dining set in a grand Neoclassical building beside the Gallery of Modern Art, this place celebrates the best of Scottish produce enriched with international influences. *glaschurestaurant.co.uk; noon-11pm*

Pub Food

Bar 91 **€**
16 F3

This buzzing gastro-pub serves well above average pub grub, with pavement tables ideal for people-watching. *bar91. co.uk; 11am-midnight Tue-Sat, from 9am Sat & Sun*

Soulsa Bar & Kitchen **€**
17 D3

Set in the Trades Hall, this cordial bar has real soul, with a range of dishes inspired by southern USA. Regular soul DJs and open-mic sessions. *soulsabar.co.uk; 10am-midnight*

Tapas

Brutti Compadres **€€**
18 C3

Hidden away in a courtyard between Miller and Virginia streets, this stylish tapas bar cooks the best nachos in town. *bruttieompadres.com;*

noon-1am Tue-Sat, from 10am Sun

Pizza

Paesano Pizza
 C2

A back-to-basics eatery that does really tasty pizzas in traditional Neapolitan style. Add some cheap Italian wines, a couple of salads and that's it. Great value. *paesanopizza.co.uk; noon-10.30pm Sun-Thu, to midnight Fri & Sat*

Indian

Dakhin
20 F3

This South Indian restaurant is a refreshing change from most of the city's curry scene. Dishes include dosas (thin rice-based crepes) and a yummy variety of fragrant coconut-based curries. *dakhin.com; noon-2pm & 5-10.30pm Mon-Fri, 1-10.30pm Sat & Sun*

Drinking

Pubs

BrewDog Glasgow Merchant City
21 E3

Brewdog's zingy beers are matched by an upbeat attitude, so this bar was always going to be a fun place; 25 taps run quality craft beer from morning till night. *brewdog.com; 11am-midnight Mon-Fri, from 10am Sat & Sun*

Babbity Bowster
22 G4

One of the city centre's most charming pubs, this handsome spot is perfect for a tranquil daytime drink, particularly in the adjoining beer garden. There's a regular folk music scene here. *babbitybowster.com; noon-midnight*

Blackfriars of Bell St
23 F4

One of the Merchant City's most relaxed and atmospheric pubs, Blackfriars' friendly staff and regular live music make it special. Buzzy and inclusive. *blackfriarsglasgow.co.uk; noon-midnight*

Bars

Spiritualist
24 C3

The high-ceilinged interior of this upmarket bar (a former library) is stunningly attractive, and it's a great place for an evening cocktail or gin and tonic. *thespiritualistglasgow.com; 4pm-midnight Wed, from noon Thu-Sat, noon-11pm Sun*

Bar Gandolfi
See **10** G4

Above the cafe of the same name (p90), this little gem is far from the boisterous Merchant Square pubs opposite. Pared-back wooden stools and tables, and offbeat art exhibitions create a relaxing space for a quality cocktail. *cafegandolfi.com; noon-midnight*

Corinthian Club
See **2** D2

A breathtaking domed ceiling and majestic chandeliers make this casino club a special space. Originally a banking hall, this lavish building's main bar is an extravaganza of ornate plasterwork and gilded cornices. *thecorinthianclub.co.uk; noon-10pm Thu, to 3am Fri & Sat, to 8pm Sun*

Artà
25 G4

This place is a tad OTT with its Mediterranean-villa decor – it really does have to be seen to be believed. Despite the luxury, it's got a relaxed vibe and makes a decent cocktail. *arta.co.uk; 5pm-midnight Thu, to 3am Fri, noon-3am Sat*

Gay

The Underground

 E2

Downstairs on cosmopolitan John St, the Underground hosts a relaxed crowd and, crucially, a free jukebox. You'll be listening to indie rather than Abba here. *facebook.com/ undergroundglasgo; 6pm-midnight Mon-Fri, from noon Sat, from 2pm Sun*

Katie's Bar

 E2

With an easily missed entrance, this basement bar is a friendly LGBTIQ+ pub with a pool table and regular gigs at weekends. It's a pleasant, low-key space to start off the night. *katiesbar.co.uk; 3pm-midnight Mon-Thu, from noon Fri & Sat, from 12.30pm Sun*

Speakeasy

 E2

Laid back and welcoming bar that starts out pub-like and gets louder with gay anthem DJs as the night progresses. Entry is free and it serves food until 9pm, so it's a good all-rounder. *speakeasy glasgow.co.uk; 8pm-1am Thu, 6pm-3am Fri & Sat, 8pm-3am Sun*

AXM

 D3

This popular Manchester club's Glasgow branch is a cheery spot, not too scene-y, with all welcome. It's a fun place to finish off a night out. *facebook .com/axmclubglasgow; 10pm-4am Fri & Sat*

Delmonica's

 D3

A popular gay bar with a good mix of ages and orientations. It's a pleasant spot for a quiet drink during the afternoon, but it packs out in the evenings when bingo, quizzes, drag shows and other events keep things lively. *delmonicas.co.uk; 2pm-1am Mon-Thu, from noon Fri-Sun*

Polo Lounge

D3

One of the city's principal gay venues. The downstairs Polo Club and Club X areas fill up on weekends, when bouncers can be strict. Just the upstairs bars open on other nights; one of them, the Riding Room, has cabaret shows. *pologlasgow. co.uk; 9pm-3am Sun-Thu, 7pm-4am Fri & Sat*

Shopping

Malls

Argyll Arcade

 A3

This historic arcade is quite a sight with its end-to-end jewellery and watch shops. Top-hatted doorpeople greet nervously excited couples shopping for diamond rings. *argyll-arcade.com; 10am-6pm Mon-Wed, 8.30am-6.30pm Thu, 8am-6pm Fri & Sat, 10am-5.30pm Sun*

Princes Square

 A3

Set in a magnificent Victorian square with elaborate ironwork and an exuberant peacock facade, this place has lots of beauty and fashion outlets and a good selection of restaurants and cafes. *princessquare. co.uk; shops 10am-6pm*

St Enoch Centre

B5

Huge glass-roofed shopping centre marking the southern end of Glasgow's shopping mile. Among its many outlets is a branch of Hamleys, the historic London toy store.

*st-enoch.com; 9am-6pm
Mon-Sat, from 10am Sun*

Vintage

Mr Ben

 E6

Cute place that's one of Glasgow's best destinations for vintage clothing, with a great selection of brands like Fred Perry, as well as more glam choices and even outdoor gear. *mrbenretroclothing. com; noon-5pm Wed-Fri, from 10.30am Sat, from 12.30pm Sun*

Art

Glasgow Print Studio

 E5

This well-designed gallery always features high-quality exhibitions and limited-edition etchings and prints. The entrance is on King St. *glasgowprintstudio.co.uk; 10am-5.30pm Tue-Sat*

Street Level Photoworks

 E5

Fine photography exhibitions are allied with a programme of courses and workshops here. There's also an entrance on King St. *streetlevelphotoworks. org; noon-5pm Tue-Sun*

Music

Monorail

See F6

This indie record shop has a carefully curated selection of alternative and experimental rock, punk, reggae, soul and jazz. It shares space with Mono (p90), a vegan cafe, so you can browse while your food is prepared. *monorailmusic.com; 11am-7pm Mon-Sat, from noon Sun*

Record Fayre

 F5

A back-to-basics music shop that's been around for years and is worth checking out for its well-priced secondhand vinyl. *facebook.com/ recordfayre; 11am-5pm Tue, from 10am Wed-Sat*

Adult

Luke & Jack

 D3

With a range of saucy items that you might not want your mother to see, this shop is a favourite with the gay community but there's plenty here for everyone, from humorous novelties to fetish gear. *facebook.com/ lukeandjack; 11am-6pm Mon-Sat, noon-5pm Sun*

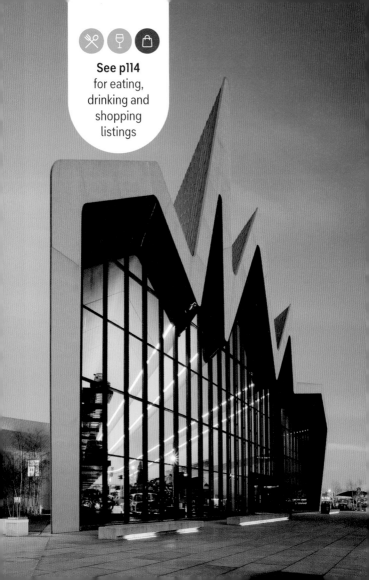

See p114
for eating,
drinking and
shopping
listings

Explore
Southside & the Clyde

Once a thriving shipbuilding area, the River Clyde sank into dereliction post-war but has been subject to extensive rejuvenation. Beyond it, the Southside is a busy web of roads dotted with sizeable parks. It's an intriguingly cosmopolitan part of Glasgow, with an up-and-coming food scene and thriving cultural centres; excellent attractions are also peppered across it. The two principal sights on the Clyde, the Riverside Museum and the Glasgow Science Centre, are family-friendly affairs that could absorb children (and adults) for several hours each, particularly the latter. It's under a mile's walk between them via the Clydeside Distillery.

Getting around

Bike
There are NextBike public bike hire stations all along the Clyde Walkway, linking the city centre to Riverside Museum and Cuningar Loop.

Bus
Buses have the best coverage of the Southside, with services 3, 4, 38 and 57 running along Pollokshaws Rd.

Subway
The subway is useful for linking Govan with the city centre and West End.

Train
The Cathcart Circle Line from Glasgow Central is handy for reaching Hampden (Mount Florida Station) and Holmwood House (Cathcart Station).

★

THE BEST

ART COLLECTION Burrell Collection (p98)

PANORAMIC VIEWS Glasgow Tower (p104)

FAMILY-FRIENDLY MUSEUM Riverside Museum (p102)

RIVER CRUISE PS Waverly (p112)

ART NOUVEAU ARCHITECTURE House for an Art Lover (p106)

Riverside Museum (p102)

For more see

★ Top Experiences p98
★ Experiences p110
✕ Eating p114
🍷 Drinking p115
🛍 Shopping p115

0 ——— 1 km
0 ——— 0.5 miles

N

☆ Seaforce Powerboats 1
🏛 Riverside Museum 2
① Govan Stones
Govan-Partick Bridge
Ⓢ Govan
River Kelvin
Clydeside Expwy
Govan Rd
Ibrox Ⓢ
Broomloan Rd
Whitefield Rd
Edmiston Dr
Bellahouston Park
● House for an Art Lover
M77

☆ Clydeside Distillery 6
🏛 7
☆ PS Waverley 8
Glasgow Science Centre
SEC Armadillo 10
Bell's Bridge
Millennium Bridge
Pacific Dr
Festival Park
OVO Hydro 9
Govan Rd
Cessnock Ⓢ
Paisley Rd West
M8

Kelvingrove Park
Royal Tce
Sauchiehall St
Berkeley St
Elderslie St
St Vincent St
Argyle St
Finnieston St
Clydeside Expwy
Elliot St
River Clyde
Anderston Quay
Broomielaw
Kingston Bridge
Seaward St
Portman St
Kinning Park Ⓢ
Paisley Rd
M8
M8
St Andrew's Dr

N Charing Cross
North St
M8
Ⓐ Anderston
Argyle St
Waterloo St
Central Station ⓐ
Ⓐ Argyle St
West St
Commerce St
Morrison St
Kingston St
Scotland St
Shields Rd Ⓢ
● Scotland Street School 13
Kingston St
Eglinton St
Bridge St
M74

St Enoch 🏛
Buchanan St
Clyde St
St Enoch Ⓢ
Bridge St Ⓢ
Borders St
Citizens Theatre 🎭

F 1
E
D
C
B
A
1
2
3
4

Scottish Football Museum

Cathcart Rd
Aikenhead Rd
Calder St
Crosshill
Pollokshaws Rd
M74
Victoria Rd
Calder St
Dixon Ave
Queens Dr
Mount Florida
Prospecthill Rd
Battlefield Rd
Langside Rd

Tramway
Pollokshields East
St Andrew's Dr
Albert Dr
Nithsdale Rd
Pollokshields West
Darnley Rd
Pollokshaws Rd
Queen's Park
Queens Park
Minard Rd
Langside Ave
See Enlargement

Crossmyloof
Kilmarnock Rd
Pollokshaws Rd
Pollokshaws East

Maxwell Park
St Andrew's Dr
Albert Dr
Shelbrooke Ave
Maxwell Dr

Dumbreck
Nithsdale Rd
Dumbreck Rd
Maxwell Ave
Sherbrooke Ave
M77
Dumbreck Rd
Burrell Collection
Dumbreck Rd

Queen's Park
Pollokshaws Rd
Langside Ave
Waverley St
Minard Rd
Norham St
Fanfoot St
Kilmarnock Rd
Abbot St
Moss-side Rd
Deanston Dr

100 m
0

Burrell Collection

Donated to the city by wealthy industrialist Sir William Burrell, this internationally significant art collection found itself homeless until an award-winning museum was built in Glasgow's Pollok Country Park in 1983. Following a six-year renovation and expansion, the Burrell Collection reopened to much fanfare in 2022.

MAP P96, **A6**

PLANNING TIP

It's worth spending a half day here, enjoying lunch in the cafe and taking the time to wander the woodland trails in surrounding Pollok Country Park.

Scan for practical information.

Entrance Hall

Burrell's idiosyncratic collection of some 9000 objects takes in everything from Chinese porcelain and medieval furniture to 16th-century tapestries and Impressionist paintings. It's not so big as to be overwhelming, and the stamp of the collector lends it an intriguing coherence. The centrepiece of the entrance hall is the **Warwick Vase** (pictured right), a monumental marble sculpture in the shape of a drinking vessel decorated with bunches of grapes and images of Bacchus, god of wine. It was unearthed in fragments in the garden of Emperor Hadrian's Villa near Rome in the 18th century; after being restored it was displayed at Warwick Castle until its acquisition by the Burrell Collection.

Rodin Bronzes

Burrell greatly admired French sculptor Auguste Rodin, and his collection includes 14 of his bronzes. **The Thinker** (1880–81), among the world's most recognisable sculptures, sits beneath the mezzanine off the entrance hall. One of 28 bronze casts still in existence, it depicts the figure of medieval Italian poet Dante Alighieri, supposedly pondering his epic poem *The Divine Comedy*. Less well-known but equally striking is **Eve After The Fall** (1880–81), part of the same commission; she stands in the furthest corner of the ground-floor galleries.

SOUTHSIDE & THE CLYDE
EXPLORE

The Burrells

A magnificent 16th-century **carved stone doorway** from Hornby Castle in North Yorkshire leads from the entrance hall into the ground-floor galleries. To the right you'll find a room titled **The Burrells**, a recreation of the Burrell family home at Hutton Castle in Berwickshire. Furniture, documents and cleverly designed interactive displays reveal the people and places that gave rise to the collection. Burrell didn't only collect art from the past, but also purchased pioneering contemporary pieces during his own lifetime, in the late 19th and early 20th centuries.

French Art

Burrell was a noted collector of late 19th-century French art, including paintings by Jean-Baptiste-Camille Corot, Jean-François Millet, Édouard Manet and Paul Cézanne. Among more than 20 works by Edgar Degas, you will find **The Rehearsal**, a modern composition full of odd and intriguing detail, and the vivid pastel rendering of **The Red Ballet Skirts** (pictured below). Cézanne's colourful **Château de Médan** has a fascinating history – it depicts the house of his friend, the writer Émile Zola, and was first owned by painter Paul Gauguin; Burrell bought it from an art dealer who shared a Paris apartment with Vincent Van Gogh.

Scottish Art

Burrell was an important collector of the group of early 20th-century Post-Impressionist artists known as the **Scottish Colourists** (p122), influenced by French painters such as Cézanne and

Matisse. Their most prominent member, Samuel John Peploe (1871–1935) is famous for his still-life paintings – look for his stylised study of **Pink Roses**. Burrell was friends with Sir John Lavery (1856–1941), an Irish painter who was known for his society portraits. The collection includes a stunning full-length portrait of Sir William's sister, **Miss Mary Burrell**, widely held to be one of Lavery's finest paintings.

Tapestry Galleries
Visitors will find their own favourite part of the museum, but the exquisite tapestry galleries are outstanding. Intricate stories capturing life in medieval Europe are woven into staggering wall-size pieces dating from the 13th to 16th centuries. The highlight is the spectacular French tapestry of 1525 entitled **Fight between a Falcon and a Heron**, an aristocratic hunting scene.

Chinese Art
The Burrell houses one of the most significant collections of Chinese art in the UK, ranging from the Neolithic period to the Qing Dynasty. A beautiful jade amulet dating from around 2800 BCE shares space with a priceless, blue-and-white, 14th-century (Ming Dynasty) **Meiping Vase** decorated with a five-clawed dragon above magic fungus-shaped clouds. Nearby is a huge white porcelain **fishbowl**, created for the emperor during the Qing Dynasty, decorated with red and blue paintings of fish and flowers.

Makers Galleries
Don't forget to investigate the first-floor Makers Galleries, where half a dozen exhibits celebrate the skills and techniques involved in creating, restoring and conserving the works of art in the collection. Learn how pastel crayons are made, how they are used, and how Edgar Degas used them to great effect in creating his atmospheric painting **Jockeys in the Rain**.

QUICK BREAK
The museum's self-service Burrell Restaurant serves a good range of Scottish-sourced dishes including sandwiches, salads and small plates (last orders for hot food at 3.15pm).

★ TOP EXPERIENCE

Riverside Museum

This impressive modern building owes its striking curved forms to late British-Iraqi architect Zaha Hadid, and houses the Riverside Museum, celebrating Scotland's outstanding contribution to the manufacture of ships, railway locomotives and motor cars, and inventions ranging from the bicycle to the steamboat.

MAP P96, **A1**

PLANNING TIP

The transport museum fills with families at weekends; visit on a weekday if you can. Although the museum is free to enter, the neighbouring Tall Ship *Glenlee* charges for admission.

Scan for practical information.

The Building

Set on the site of one of Glasgow's most prominent former shipyards, A & J Inglis, the museum was designed by Zaha Hadid. Its two facades have great visual impact, with the building's zinc cladding zig-zagging across the top of vast dark-glass windows.

Main Street

This recreated cobbled street is an atmospheric display of shops as they would have appeared in the late 19th and early 20th centuries. Pop in to admire the saddler, pawnbrokers, portrait photographer and more. There's a fascinating exhibit on **Glasgow's subway**, the world's third oldest underground railway after London and Budapest, opened in 1896. Take a seat in one of the original wood-panelled coaches, which was in service from 1898 to 1977.

Wall of Cars

Three levels of motor vehicles are dramatically displayed on one wall of the museum, including Sir William Burrell's **Rolls-Royce Phantom ll**. The collection highlights Scottish-made vehicles, such as the **Hillman Imp**. All around are vintage trams and electric trolleybuses, a massive South African **steam locomotive** built in Glasgow in 1945, and a model of the **QEII**, the last great ocean liner to be built on the Clyde, launched in 1967.

UNGVARI ATTILA/SHUTTERSTOCK ©, ARCHITECT: ZAHA HADID

World's Oldest Bicycle

The small upstairs floor can be a retreat from the downstairs hubbub. The key sight here is a pedal-powered **bicycle** dating from 1846, considered the oldest surviving example in the world. There is still some controversy over who invented it – Kirkpatrick Macmillan or Gavin Dalzell – but both were Scottish. Nearby displays detail Scotland's contribution to the invention of the earliest **steamships**.

The Tall Ship

Docked outside the museum, the elegant three-masted sailing ship **Glenlee** (*thetallship.com; adult/child £4.50/2.70*) was built on the Clyde and launched in 1896. On board are three decks to explore, with family-friendly displays about the vessel's history, restoration and shipboard life during its heyday.

QUICK BREAK
The museum and Tall Ship both have a cafe. The nearest alternative is the **Clydeside Cafe** at the Clydeside Distillery, a 10-minute walk away along the riverside.

Glasgow Science Centre

The futuristic Glasgow Science Centre on the banks of the Clyde is packed full of brilliantly interactive displays and exhibits about all fields of science and is huge fun for all ages. You could easily spend half a day here discovering everything there is to see and do.

MAP P96, **B2**

PLANNING TIP
There's an IMAX cinema here too; check the session times for this, the planetarium and any special events ahead of your visit.

Scan for practical information.

A Question of Perception

On the 1st floor, these experiences could be called Question of Deception as the interactive exhibits test all your senses. There are some great illusions here; all ages will find something to delight or perplex them. Check out the **Ames Room**, where kids can appear taller than their parents.

Powering the Future

The 2nd floor explores electricity generation and the 'energy trilemma' of affordability, security of supply and environmental sustainability, where tackling one issue may affect the other two. Grab a computer terminal and play the **MyDECC50 simulation**, which allows you to be energy minister for a day and see the effects of your decisions.

Bodyworks

On the top floor, this all-ages display provides detailed information about the human body and modern medicine. You're bound to discover something that you didn't know, but there's plenty of fun to be had here too, with numerous hadns on displays. Compare your grip strength to other visitors.

Glasgow Tower

An additional ticket is needed for access to this high-tech rotating tower; at 127m tall, with an **observation deck** at 105m, it's the tallest free-

BINSON CALFORT/SHUTTERSTOCK ©

standing rotating structure in the world, capable of turning 360 degrees. Its 500-tonne weight is carried on a single phosphor-bronze ball bearing the diameter of a bicycle wheel. The 2½-minute trip to the top offers terrific views of the Clyde and across the city. Tablets in the viewing cabin let you zoom in on what you are looking at, while guides are on hand to explain the technology and point out places of interest.

Planetarium

Accessed via the 1st floor with an additional ticket, the Planetarium has a 15m-wide dome screening various immersive shows suitable for a range of ages, from discovering the night sky to Pink Floyd's *Dark Side of the Moon*. You don't need a ticket to take a stroll through the solar system in the **Space Zone** exhibition in the foyer.

QUICK BREAK
There's a cafe in the museum, as well as a coffee shop in the IMAX cinema. There are no other eateries within easy walking distance.

★ TOP EXPERIENCE

House for an Art Lover

Charles Rennie Mackintosh entered a portfolio of drawings for an international architecture competition run by a German interior design magazine in 1901. The drawings – for 'a grand house in a thoroughly modern style' – lay unrealised until the City of Glasgow completed the building to Mackintosh's design in 1996.

MAP P96, **A4**

PLANNING TIP

House for an Art Lover is in Bellahouston Park; take bus 9 from Buchanan St bus station to the Palace of Art stop. It's occasionally closed for private events; check online.

Scan for practical information.

Main Hall

Heading upstairs from the reception you arrive in the main hall, a double-height room with tall windows and a pillared balcony. The effect is of soft northern light and soaring space, with characteristic Mackintosh details such as the rose motif in the pewter panels on the pillars and the stained glass around the fireplace and in the doors to the music room.

Dining Room

The dining room is a sombre space of dark oak panelling and furniture, designed to provide an unfussy backdrop for the bright, fashionable clothes of the diners. There are splashes of colour from stencilled roses, the architect's favourite symbol, and a series of 24 gesso panels depicting the flower's life story.

Music Room

This is the heart of the house, an extravaganza in white (Mackintosh's buildings were typically dark on the north side, and bright on the south). The room (pictured right)is flooded with sunlight, mimicking a forest glade with willow motifs and Tree of Life imagery. The piano (you can play it) is surrounded by outrageously Art Nouveau decoration; note the kissing doves above.

Oval Room

This understated room was designed for ladies

to retire to after dinner. It's the only room that was drawn only in plan, with no perspective view, meaning the builders had to do a lot of research.

Margaret Macdonald Room

Mackintosh worked closely with his wife Margaret on the design of the house and her influence is evident, especially in the rose motif which links the different rooms. The displays here detail the techniques used to create the artwork in the house.

Interpretation Centre

Copies of Mackintosh's original drawings are on display on the balcony above the main hall, and computers allow you to examine the designs more closely and learn about the house's history. The entire building's design was based on just 14 drawings.

QUICK BREAK
The **Art Lover's Cafe** is set on the ground floor of the house and spills out onto a sunny terrace. It makes a relaxing spot for breakfast or brunch.

WALKING TOUR

Walk The Clyde

Redevelopment has created pleasant walkways along the banks of the River Clyde, passing reminders of Glasgow's heyday as a hotbed of the shipbuilding industry. This walk links the oldest pedestrian bridge over the Clyde (1853) with the newest (2024). Both start and finish are easily reached via the subway.

START	END	LENGTH
Portland Street Bridge	Govan-Partick Bridge	3 miles; 1½ hours

1 Oldest Bridge

Start at the north end of the Portland Street Bridge, an elegant wrought-iron suspension bridge with sandstone towers, opened in 1853. Head downstream on the Clyde Walkway, passing beneath two road bridges and the noisy railway bridge serving Central Station. Go up the ramp and cross King George V Bridge to the financial district.

2 Squiggly Bridge

Continue along the south bank of the Clyde, flanked by the offices of financial businesses, and recross the river via the Tradeston Bridge, opened in 2009 and nicknamed the Squiggly Bridge for its sinuous shape.

3 Squinty Bridge

Rejoin the Clyde Walkway and pass beneath the Kingston Bridge, which carries the M8 motorway, to reach the Clyde Arc (2006), a graceful arched road bridge nicknamed the Squinty Bridge because of its angled crossing.

4 Hidden Tunnel

On the right is a circular red-brick building known as the Rotunda with a matching one on the far side of the river. These mark the 24m-deep lift shafts serving the Glasgow Harbour Tunnel, built in 1896 for horse-drawn vehicles and pedestrians (now closed).

5 Finnieston Crane

Nearby is the giant 53m-tall cantilever Finnieston Crane, a symbol of Glasgow's heritage as an industrial port. From 1932 to 1969 it was used to lift railway locomotives and other heavy machinery onto cargo ships.

6 Bell's Bridge

You now enter the Scottish Events Campus (SEC), dominated by the distinctive interlocking ships' hulls of the SEC Armadillo (1997), designed by Norman Foster. Cross Bell's Bridge, a cable-stayed cantilever footbridge built in 1988 for the Glasgow Garden Festival.

7 Millennium Bridge

Head towards the Glasgow Science Centre past the headquarters of BBC Scotland and recross the river via the Millennium Bridge (2002). Continue downstream past the Clydeside Distillery (the cafe here is good for a coffee stop).

8 Newest Bridge

Your walk ends at the Riverside Museum, where the Clyde's newest crossing, the Govan-Partick Bridge (2024), gives easy access to the Govan Stones (p110) and Fairfield Heritage (p111).

EXPERIENCES

Lay a Hand on History at the Govan Stones ANCIENT CARVED STONES

MAP: ❶ P96 A1

Govan Old Church, a Victorian building on the south bank of the River Clyde, occupies one of Scotland's earliest places of Christian worship, and is home to the Govan Stones (*thegovanstones.org.uk*; admission free), a remarkable collection of ancient carvings. There has been a church here for around 1500 years, and during the 9th to 11th centuries this was the burial place of the kings of Strathclyde. The church is dedicated to St Constantine, a Christian martyr who was killed by marauding Vikings in 876; his beautifully carved stone sarcophagus is on display here, along with a remarkable collection of **Viking 'hogsback' gravestones** discovered in the churchyard. The Govan-Partick Bridge allows easy pedestrian access to the church (closed November to March) from the Riverside Museum.

See the City from the Water BOAT TRIP

MAP: ❷ P96 A1

If a visit to the Tall Ship at the Riverside Museum has whetted your appetite for all things nautical, sign up for a trip with **Seaforce Powerboats** (*seaforcepowerboats.co.uk*; *adult/child from £20/16*). Departing from the quay outside the museum, these high-speed RIBs will take you on anything from a 20-minute thrash around the nearby Clydeside sights – the Science Centre, the Finnieston Crane, the Clyde Arc bridge and the old shipyards – to a 45-minute blast downstream to the spectacular Erskine Bridge. Trips run year-round but are dependent on weather and water conditions; call ahead.

Discover 'Greek' Thomson at Holmwood House HISTORIC HOUSE

MAP: ❸ P96 C8

Think Glasgow architecture and you think Charles Rennie Mackintosh. But Alexander Thomson (1817–75) may be the greatest Glasgow architect you've never heard of. More prolific than Mackintosh (many of his Glasgow buildings survive – see the Central Glasgow walking tour, p42), his designs were considered unusual at the time but achieved international recognition. **Holmwood House** (*nts.org.uk*; *adult/child £8.50/6*) was built for James Couper, a papermill owner, in 1858, and is considered to be Thomson's finest domestic building. The house revels in Thomson's signature motifs of Ancient Greek architecture, including geometric friezes, Ionic columns, ornate cupolas and frescoes depicting scenes from Homer's *Iliad*. The entrance is on Netherlee Rd, a 15-minute walk south of Cathcart train station (trains from Glasgow Central run four times an hour and take 15 minutes).

Hear the Hampden Roar
FOOTBALL STADIUM

MAP: **4** P96 **F8**

Hampden Park, Scotland's national football stadium and home pitch of Queen's Park, is hallowed ground for Scottish football fans. When built in 1903 it was the world's biggest stadium, and holds the European record for attendance – a crowd of 149,415 watched Scotland v England in 1937. The noise of cheering fans could be heard across the city, and became known as the 'Hampden Roar'.

One of the highlights of the **guided tour** (*scottishfootballmuseum.org.uk; adult/child £16/9*) is running out into the arena with a recording of the Hampden roar ringing in your ears. The hour-long tour includes the dressing rooms, decorated with shirts worn by famous players, and a visit to the Scottish Football Museum, where you can see the world's oldest football trophy.

To reach Hampden Park, take a train from Glasgow Central to Mount Florida station.

Learn About the Clyde's Shipbuilding Heritage
SHIPBUILDING MUSEUM

MAP: **5** P96 **A1**

In the early 20th century the Clyde was the greatest shipbuilding river in the world, with over 100,000 workers employed across more than 40 shipbuilding yards. The industry declined from the 1950s onward, and today only two yards remain. Fairfield Heritage (*fairfieldgovan.co.uk; admission free*), housed in the magnificently restored Victorian offices of the Fairfield Shipbuilding and Engineering Company, chronicles this fascinating history – learn how Fairfield built some of the fastest transatlantic ocean liners of the 19th century, and continues to build warships for the British government. The museum is a short walk west of Govan Old Church.

Savour a Dram at Clydeside Distillery
MALT WHISKY DISTILLERY

MAP: **6** P96 **B2**

It's great to see this old pumphouse by the Clyde being put to good use as the **Clydeside**

QUEEN'S PARK FC

Queen's Park FC, founded in 1867, is Scotland's oldest football club, and 10th oldest in the world. Hampden Park has been their home ground since 1873; remarkably, the team remained wholly amateur until 2019. They dominated Scottish football in the early days, winning the Scottish Cup 10 times between 1874 and 1893. The Scottish Cup itself is the oldest footballing trophy in the world, dating from 1873; although England's FA Cup competition is older by three years, its current trophy dates only from 1911. The genuine Scottish Cup is on display in Hampden's museum (the current holders are given a replica).

Distillery (*theclydeside.com; tour £18.50 per person*) run by proper whisky folk. It's an impressive set-up, with stills overlooking the river (don't worry, the water comes from Loch Katrine, not the Cylde). The engaging one-hour tour has some Clydeside history thrown in and includes a tasting of three malts. There's also a cafe and well-stocked whisky shop.

Go Bouldering at Cuningar Loop

ADVENTURE PLAYGROUND

MAP: **7** P96 **F5**

Set in a looping bend of the River Clyde on the city's southeastern edge, the popular **Cuningar Loop** woodland park (*forestryandland. gov.scot; admission free*) offers a range of outdoor activities. There's an adventure playground with rope swings, a sand pit, monkey bars and climbing frames made out of logs that will test the mettle of the most adventurous kids, plus a series of bike trails that include a challenging pump track. The highlight is Scotland's first (and so far only) **outdoor bouldering park**, with nine artificial concrete resin boulders up to 4m high, offering

problems graded for everyone from beginner to expert – check out the descents first as some are a little intimidating.

Take a Cruise 'Doon the Watter'

BOAT TRIP

MAP: **8** P96 **B2**

Taking a trip 'doon the watter' (ie 'down the water', meaning along the River Clyde) was a mainstay of Glasgow working-class holidays from the late 19th century until the 1950s. Dozens of steamboats large and small took day trippers and holidaymakers from the Broomielaw Quay in central Glasgow to the various ports and resorts along the shores of the Firth of Clyde.

The PS *Waverley* (*waverleyexcursions.co.uk; £40-57 per person*) – the last surviving sea-going paddle steamer in the world, built in 1947 – maintains the tradition, with daily summer cruises from Glasgow to the islands of Bute, Great Cumbrae and Arran, and the mainland towns of Largs, Tighnabruaich, Tarbert and Ardrishaig. Departures are from the Glasgow Science Centre Quay; check the website for detailed timetables.

--- **CLYDE WALKWAY** ---

The riverside Clyde Walkway (*scotlandsgreattrails.com*) is a foot and cycle path that runs from Glasgow upriver to the Falls of Clyde near New Lanark, some 40 miles away; the Glasgow tourist office has a good leaflet pack detailing different sections of the trail. Grab a NextBike from any public hire station and tackle the easy six-mile stretch from Riverside Museum to Cuningar Loop (40 minutes each way) to try your hand at bouldering.

See a Gig at the Armadillo ENTERTAINMENT

The Scottish Events Campus (SEC) is an entertainment complex on the banks of the Clyde just west of the city centre. The main arena, and the busiest entertainment venue in Scotland, is the 14,500-capacity **OVO Hydro** (MAP: **9** P96 C2; *sec.co.uk*). This spectacular modern building is a popular option for big-name concerts and shows: everyone from Kylie Minogue and Elton John to Billie Eilish and Charli XCX have played here. Check the website to see what's on during you trip.

But the SEC's most distinctive feature is the **SEC Armadillo** (MAP: **10** P96 C2), a 3000-seat venue that provides a stage for conferences, stand-up comedians, tribute bands and smaller gigs. Originally called the Clyde Auditorium, it was designed to look like interlocking ships' hulls in a nod to the area's shipbuilding heritage, but the people of Glasgow just called it the Armadillo, and the name stuck.

Visit a Bit of Dramatic History HISTORICAL THEATRE

The **Citizens Theatre** (MAP: **11** P96 F4; *citz.co.uk*) has been centre stage on Glasgow's performing arts scene since it was founded in 1943. Based in a Victorian theatre built in 1878 in the Gorbals district (once notorious for its slums), its mission has always been to bring affordable, world-class theatre to the citizens of Glasgow. Famous names who have trod the boards here include Moira Shearer, Pierce Brosnan, Rupert Everett, Celia Imrie, Alan Rickman, Glenda Jackson, Gary Oldman and Sam Heughan.

Since 2019 the company has performed at the **Tramway** (MAP: **12** P96 E5; *trammway.org*) arts venue while its home theatre building undergoes a major restoration – the Citizens is famous as having the oldest functioning stage machinery in the UK, and retains its original proscenium arch stage. The theatre is set to reopen in 2025 – check their social media for the latest news.

Go Back to School on Scotland Street MACKINTOSH ARCHITECTURE

MAP: **13** P96 D4

Charles Rennie Mackintosh's famous **Scotland Street School** (*glasgowlife.org.uk*) looks a bit forlorn these days, on a windswept industrial street south of the river. Built in 1906, it functioned as a school until 1979, then housed a museum of education that closed during the Covid pandemic. There are plans to restore the building as part museum, part nursery and childcare facility – meanwhile, it's worth a visit to view the wonderful Mackintosh facade (if it's not covered in scaffolding).

Best Places for...

❸ Budget **❸❸** Midrange **❸❸❸** Top End

Eating

Italian

Oro ❸❸
 C8

Classic Italian cuisine has made Oro a stalwart of the Southside dining scene for more than 20 years. Head chef Domenico Crolla is famed for creating portraits on his pizzas. *oro. restaurant; noon-11pm*

Errol's Hot Pizza ❸
⑮ E6

There are only a handful of tables at this hole-in-the-wall pizza joint in the up-and-coming neighbourhood of Govanhill. Book in advance for the best pizza in Glasgow. *instagram.com/ errolshotpizzashop; 5-9.30pm Thu-Sun*

Pub Grub

Corona Bar & Kitchen ❸
⑯ B7

Originally built in 1913, this ornately decorated pub is a local landmark, serving good-quality pub food. *corona-bar.com; 11am-9.30pm*

Asian

Chawp Pet Noi ❸❸
 A8

Best book a table (or order a takeaway) as this friendly place is both small and deservedly popular (there are no bookings on Fridays and Saturdays). Authentic Thai food served with flair. *chawppetnoi.co.uk; 4-9.15pm*

Ranjit's Kitchen ❸
⑱ E6

A Sikh family brings authentic home-cooked flavours from the Punjab to this little Southside restaurant. *ranjitskitchen. com; noon-8.30pm Tue-Sun*

Little Hoi An ❸
⑲ E6

This cute little kitchen has just a few tables, some outside, and serves classic Vietnamese street food – sticky salt'n'chilli pork belly, prawn or tofu summer rolls with peanut dip, coconut curries and, of course, fragrant pho. BYOB. *facebook .com/littlehoianglasgow; 5-9.30pm Wed & Thu, 5-10pm Fri & Sat*

Seafood

Salt & Vinegar ❸
⑳ B7

A cut above your average chippie, this place serves not only haddock and chips but also lobster ravioli, fried calamari, sea bass and scallops, as well as fresh pasta and risotto dishes, to sit in or take away. *saltandvinegarglas gow.com; 11.30am-10pm*

Cafes

Brooklyn Cafe ❸
㉑ B7

Classic Scottish-Italian cafe that's been around since 1931, run by the Pelosi family. From breakfast fry-ups to Tuscan grilled cheese to American-style club sandwiches. *facebook.com/ Brooklyn1931; 9am-4pm*

Art Lover's Cafe ❸
㉒ A4

The cafe at **House for an Art Lover** (p106) majors in quality breakfast and lunch dishes,

See p96 for map of locations

plus all-day sandwiches and cakes. *houseforanartlover.co.uk; 10am-4pm*

Gusto & Relish

 23 E6

Family-friendly breakfast spot serving French toast, waffles, veggie fry-ups and baked eggs, plus locally roasted coffee, cakes and deli sandwiches. There are books, toys and games for the kids. *facebook.com/gustoandrelish; 9am-5pm Mon-Fri, from 9.30am Sat & Sun*

Drinking

Bars

Red Sky Bar

24 D2

Rooftop bar with spectacular views, stylish interiors and a relaxed ambience attracting city-centre workers for post-work pints and proseccos. *redskybar.com; noon-1am*

Rum Shack

25 E6

Near Queens Park Station, this upbeat Caribbean-themed spot serves up more than a hundred varieties of rum, backed up with a menu of Jamaican and Creole-influenced

dishes. *rumshackglasgow.com; 4-9.30pm Mon-Thu, from noon Fri-Sun*

Pubs

Clutha & Victoria Bar

26 F3

This historic 200-year-old pub near the river (Clutha is Gaelic for Clyde) continues its long tradition of hosting live music and colourful murals. *facebook.com/Cluthabar; noon-midnight Wed-Sun, from 5pm Mon & Tue*

Coffee Shops

Cafe Strange Brew

27 A8

The Southside's best coffee shop, using locally roasted Dear Green beans; leave room for the sinfully sticky desserts. *facebook.com/cafestrangebrew; 9am-4pm*

Glad Cafe

28 B7

Social enterprise cafe, thrift shop and multi-arts venue with excellent coffee, craft beers, interesting food and a laid-back bohemian vibe. *thegladcafe.co.uk; 11am-late Mon-Fri, 10am-late Sat & Sun*

Bramble

29 D7

Classic neighbourhood coffee shop on Pollok-

shaws Rd – cappuccino with chocolate flakes, waffles with ice cream. *facebook.com/bramblecafesouthside; 9am-4pm*

Shopping

Park Lane Market

30 C7

This lively market opposite Queen's Park operates on the first and last Sunday of the month, with stalls selling fashion, music, bric-a-brac and secondhand goods. *parklanemarket.co.uk; 11am-4pm Sun*

Stephen O'Neil Art

31 B7

Design gallery opposite Langside Hall on Pollokshaws Rd, selling Glasgow-themed prints, books and greetings cards. *stephenoneil.co.uk; 10am-5pm Mon-Sat, 11am-4pm Sun*

Glad Rags Thrift

32 B7

Part of the Glad Cafe complex, this not-for-profit co-op specialises in preloved clothing sourced from local donations. *facebook.com/gladragsglasgow; noon-5pm Wed & Fri-Sun, noon-7pm Thu*

See p137
for eating,
drinking and
shopping
listings

Explore
West End

As in London, the name West End evokes images of wealth and sophistication, and Glasgow's West End is no different – the term is a legacy of the Industrial Revolution when the prevailing westerly winds blew the smoke and stink of city centre industry away to the east. With its appealing studenty buzz, cool bars and cafes and bohemian swagger, the West End remains the trendiest part of town and is for many the most engaging of Glasgow's neighbourhoods. Streets of elegant terraced houses and ample parkland cover large areas of the district, which is centred around the Victorian grandeur of the University of Glasgow and Kelvingrove Art Gallery & Museum.

Getting around

On Foot
You can walk the length of Byres Rd in about 15 to 20 minutes.

Bus
From the city centre, buses 6 and 6A run along Great Western Rd, 4 along Woodlands Rd, 3 and 77 along Sauchiehall St, and 2 along Argyle St.

Subway
Get off at Kelvinbridge station for Great Western Rd, Hillhead for Byres Rd, and Kelvinhall for Kelvingrove Art Gallery & Museum.

THE BEST

ART GALLERY Kelvingrove Art Gallery & Museum (p120)

GREEN SPACE Kelvingrove Park (p134)

THEATRE EXPERIENCE A Play, a Pie and a Pint at Oràn Mór (p138)

SHOPPING Byres Rd lanes (p134)

MUSEUM Hunterian Museum (p124)

Kelvingrove Art Gallery & Museum (p120)
JEFF WHYTE/SHUTTERSTOCK ©

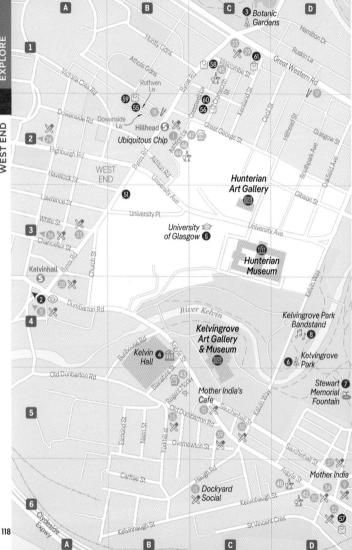

A B C D

3 Botanic Gardens

Hamilton Dr

1

Huntly Gdns

Athole Gdns

33

Ruskin La

Great Western Rd

Victoria Cres Rd

Ruthven La

58

Vinicombe St

29 61

17

59

55 18

Byres Rd

45

Cresswell La

Kersland St

Cecil St

Glasgow St

Downside Rd

Downside La

60

56

Craigoch

Southpark Ave

Oakfield Ave

Hillhead S

Great George St

Highburgh Rd

24

2

Ubiquitous Chip

47

Ashton La

44

Hunterian Art Gallery

Gibson St

WEST END

Havelock St

Byres Rd

University Ave

University Pl

51

University of Glasgow 5

University Ave

Lawrence St

White St

3

Chancellor St

23

Church St

Hunterian Museum

Kelvinhall S

28

Kelvin Way

Dumbarton Rd

2

River Kelvin

31

4

Kelvingrove Park Bandstand 8

Burnhouse Rd

Argyle St

Kelvin Hall 4

Kelvingrove Art Gallery & Museum

Kelvingrove Park 6

Old Dunbarton Rd

Blantyre St

Regent Moray St

Stewart Memorial Fountain 7

Mother India's Cafe

5

Esmond St

Nairn St

Yorkhill St

Old Dunbarton Rd

Sauchiehall Rd

25

Kelvin Way

Overnewton St

39

Sauchiehall St

23

Mother India 9

Carfrae St

Haugh Rd

48

34

15 Dockyard Social

42

59

32

6

Clydeside Expwy

Kelvinhaugh St

St Vincent Cres

57

A B C D

For more see

Top Experiences ⭐	p120
Experiences ⭐	p132
Eating 🍴	p137
Drinking 🍺	p139
Shopping 🛍	p140

Kelvin Walkway

River Kelvin

Raeberry St

Belmont St

Woodside Rd N

Napiershall St

Maryhill Rd

Kelvinbridge

Park Rd

Great Western Rd

Shish Mahal

Otago La

Gibson St

The Stand

W Princes St

Dunearn St

Woodlands Rd

Eldon St

Kelvin Walkway

Kelvingrove Park

Park Tce

Park Circus

Park

St Georges Cross

Great Western Rd

St Georges Rd

Ruthven St

Arlington Baths

Arlington St

W Princes St

Grant St

Carnarvon St

Junction 17

Lynedoch St

Woodlands Tce

Woodside Tce

Woodside Tce

M8

Royal Tce

Woodside Pl

Woodside Pl La

Elderslie St

Hill St

Garnet St

Renfrew St

Sauchiehall St

Sauchiehall St

Sauchiehall St

Berkeley St

Berkeley St

Mitchell Library

Elderslie St

Kent Rd

North St

Bath St

Charing Cross

Elmbank St

Holland St

Royal Tce

Argyle St

Bon Accord

M8

EXPLORE

WEST END

Kelvingrove Art Gallery & Museum

Built for the Glasgow International Exhibition of 1901, this red sandstone palace of culture is Scotland's most-visited free attraction, covering a huge range of subjects from archaeology to natural history in an accessible modern way. Its art collection in particular is outstanding.

MAP P118, **C4**

PLANNING TIP
You can hear the great pipe organ being played during daily recitals at 1pm Monday to Saturday, and 3pm on Sunday.

Scan for practical information.

Centre Hall

After admiring the **Kelvingrove Art Gallery & Museum** exterior, go through the doors into the vast **Centre Hall**, a spectacularly ornate confection of polished chandeliers, polychrome marble and richly carved sandstone beneath arched colonnades and vaulted ceilings, with one end dominated by a behemoth of a **concert organ** (pictured right; it has no fewer than 2889 pipes). Pick up a floor plan from the information desk at the far end of the hall. The museum is divided into two wings, one focusing on **Life** (history, archaeology and nature) and the other on **Expression** (art). Head upstairs to the South Gallery and begin with the museum's most famous item.

A Dalí Masterwork

Arguably the highlight of the whole museum hangs in a small 1st-floor room near the central atrium. Based on dreams, Salvador Dalí's **Christ of St John of the Cross** is perhaps his greatest work. Forget ridiculous moustaches and surrealist frippery: this is a serious, awesomely powerful painting. A sinewy, crucified Christ looks down through an infinity of sky and darkness to a simple fishing boat in Galilee (the landscape here was inspired by Catalonia in Spain). Dalí strapped a Hollywood stuntman to a gantry to get the musculature right.

NINA ALIZADA/SHUTTERSTOCK ©

Scottish Identity in Art

Next head into the east wing (Expression), whose atrium is filled with **Floating Heads**, a striking installation by Sophie Cave. The **Scottish Identity in Art** exhibit looks at how Scotland is portrayed on canvas, with portraits of Robert Burns, Bonnie Prince Charlie and Mary Queen of Scots. The landscapes here include some jaw-dropping depictions of Highland scenes. Standing in front of Gustave Doré's **Glen Massan**, you can almost feel the drizzle and smell the heather. David Wilkie's **The Cotter's Saturday Night** is based on the poem by Robert Burns, which you can listen to alongside it.

European Art

The next gallery shows off Kelvingrove's collection of French and European masterpieces, including works by Renoir, Gaugin and Picasso.

QUICK BREAK
There's a cafe
in the museum,
but if you fancy
something
spicier head
across Argyle
St to **Mother
India's Cafe** for
a tapas-style
selection of
Indian dishes.

Look out for **Vétheuil**, Claude Monet's quintessential Impressionist landscape, rapidly captured in just a few hours; contrast this with the less ethereal landscape by **Paul Cézanne** located alongside it. One of Dufy's famous canvases, **The Jetties at Trouville-Deauville**, also hangs in this room, as do works by many other masters including an early **Van Gogh** depicting his onetime flatmate, ginger-bearded Glaswegian art dealer Alexander Reid.

The Scottish Colourists

Next is a small gallery devoted to the Scottish Colourists, four artists working in the early decades of the 20th century who brought a French flourish of colour and light to the Scottish art scene. The highlight is **The Orange Blind** by

Francis Cadell, a typically bold and elegant portrayal of a fashionable Edinburgh salon in shades of blue, green and orange; the stylish woman in the foreground pats the chaise longue she is sitting on, as if to invite the viewer to come join her.

The Glasgow Boys

The ground-floor galleries of the east wing house a large room devoted to the Glasgow Boys. Inspired by Whistler, these artists broke with romanticism to pioneer a more modern style. Compare William Kennedy's grounded **Stirling Station** or the realism of James Guthrie's **A Funeral Service in the Highlands** with those misty Scottish landscapes upstairs. Also noteworthy in this space is Sir John Lavery's famous theatrical portrait of **Anna Pavlova**.

The Glasgow Style

You will have seen most of the paintings now, but there's plenty left to discover if you're not worn out. Try the room dedicated to Art Deco and Glasgow Style interiors and designs. 'Margaret has genius, I have only talent', said **Charles Rennie Mackintosh** of his wife, and there's a good display of her work here – particularly her exquisite gesso panels – as well as that of her sister, Frances Macdonald.

West Wing: Life

The other side of the museum, dominated by a hanging **WWII Spitfire** (pictured left), has two floors of rooms featuring impressive prehistoric and Viking-era carved stones, Egyptian grave goods and other archaeological finds. Suits of armour are cleverly placed in an exhibition about the human consequences of war, and there are some fine social history displays. The taxidermied animals downstairs are a reminder of the museum's Victorian past; **Sir Roger the elephant** was a notable Glasgow character in his day.

LEGACY OF EMPIRE
Look out for the museum's information panels, which acknowledge the origins of many of the objects on display in Glasgow's connection to the British Empire and the slave trade.

THE EXTERIOR
The building was designed in Spanish Baroque style; the elaborate north facade overlooking Kelvingrove Park is said to have been inspired by the Cathedral of Santiago de Compostela.

Hunterian Museum

The Hunterian Museum is the oldest public museum in Scotland (founded in 1807), part of one of the oldest universities in Scotland (founded in 1451). It's based around the collections of renowned former student William Hunter (1718–83), professor of anatomy and the leading obstetrician of his day.

MAP P118, **C3**

PLANNING TIP
Join a free 25-minute guided tour led by a volunteer student guide; tours start at noon Tuesday to Saturday (also 2pm Thursday and Friday) from mid-July to November.

Scan for practical information.

Roman Scotland

The Hunterian occupies the second floor of Glasgow University's Neo-gothic main building. The first hall you enter is dedicated to The Antonine Wall: Rome's Final Frontier, with an exceptional collection of Roman artefacts discovered in central Scotland. Built around 142 CE, the wall ran from the north shore of the Clyde to the Firth of Forth, marking the northernmost outpost of the empire. On display are superb examples of monumental sculpture, richly carved distance slabs that celebrated the completion of sections of the wall, beautifully decorated jugs and vases and everyday objects, including leather shoes, iron nails and gaming pieces.

Main Hall

The main hall's eclectic displays range from geology and palaeontology to archaeology and anthropology, always with a bias to objects with a Glasgow (or at least Scottish) connection. The Bearsden sharks exhibit highlights the world's most complete fossils of 330-million-year-old sharks, discovered in the local suburb of Bearsden. The fossils are so well-preserved that blood vessels, muscles and even the shark's final meal can be studied.

Medical History

The south mezzanine gallery celebrates Glasgow's contribution to medical science, including the work

SERGII FIGURNYI/SHUTTERSTOCK ©

of Joseph Lister, Professor of Surgery at Glasgow (1860–69) and pioneer of antisepsis. On show are his carbolic spray, William Hunter's original 18th-century anatomical and pathological specimens, some of the first X-ray images made by John MacIntyre (1857–1928) – who established the world's first radiology department at Glasgow Royal Infirmary – and one of the world's first ultrasound scanners.

Physics & Applied Science

The north gallery is dedicated to William Thomson, Lord Kelvin, Professor of Natural Philosophy at Glasgow for 53 years (1846–1899). Among Kelvin's many achievements, he paved the way for the transatlantic telegraph cable and the modern refrigerator; the exhibits display his original teaching models and experimental instruments.

QUICK BREAK
Head down the hill and around the corner to Gibson St where you can choose between snacks at **Left Bank** or a more substantial lunch at **Stravaigin**.

Hunterian Art Gallery & Mackintosh House

The modern campus across University Ave from Glasgow University's Gothic main building is centred on the excellent Hunterian Art Gallery, along with a recreation of the exquisite house of Charles Rennie Mackintosh and his wife, Margaret Macdonald, which used to stand nearby.

MAP P118, **C3**

PLANNING TIP
Access to the art gallery and the introductory Mackintosh exhibition beside the reception is free, but you'll need to buy a ticket to enter the Mackintosh House.

Scan for practical information.

Hunterian Art Gallery

The Hunterian's art collection is housed in a modern building across the road from the museum, part of the university's Brutalist library complex built in 1968. There's an understandable focus on Scottish art, including powerful modern works by Peter Howson, John Byrne and Joan Eardley, 19th-century society portraits by Henry Raeburn, and the distinctive still-lifes and landscapes of the Scottish Colourists, notably the Iona paintings of Francis Cadell.

A key highlight is one of the world's largest collections of James McNeill Whistler's limpid prints, drawings and paintings. Notable are the full-length portraits of his wife, *Harmony in Red*, and of Miss Ethel Philip, *Harmony in Black*. Look out, too, for William MacTaggart's impressionistic Scottish landscapes and a gem by Thomas Millie Dow.

The Mackintosh House

The construction of the art gallery and library complex in 1968 entailed the demolition of a row of terraced houses including 78 Southpark Avenue – the Glasgow home that Charles Rennie Mackintosh shared with his wife, noted designer/artist Margaret Macdonald, from 1906 to 1914. The building project included a careful reconstruction of Mackintosh's three-storey house, complete with original furniture, fixtures and fittings.

ALASTAIR WALLACE/SHUTTERSTOCK ©

Entered via the Hunterian Art Gallery, the Mackintosh House (pictured; adult/child £10/6) provides a wonderful insight into the lives and imaginations of Charles and Margaret, and it's fair to say that interior decoration was one of their strong points – the rooms feel startlingly modern even today. The quiet elegance of the hall and dining room on the ground floor give way upstairs to the visual showstopper, the breathtaking whiter-than-white drawing room and bedroom.

The Mackintosh Collection

Mackintosh and Macdonald's heirs gifted the contents of the Glasgow house to the Hunterian in 1947, along with more than 600 drawings, posters, watercolours and other artworks, just some of which are on display in this top-floor exhibition, along with a recreation of another Mackintosh interior: the bedroom at 78 Derngate, Northampton.

QUICK BREAK

It's a short walk west from the gallery to the wall-to-wall bars and restaurants of cute little Ashton Lane; we recommend **Brel** for *moules frites* and a beer.

WALKING TOUR

Walk the West End

This walk is a highlights tour of the western part of Glasgow, taking in the key shopping and eating strips as well as parks, pubs, the university and the major sights. It could be a brisk stroll to get your bearings before returning in depth, or a lazy meander that could easily occupy a day.

START	END	LENGTH
Kelvin Bridge	Kelvingrove Art Gallery	2 miles; two hours

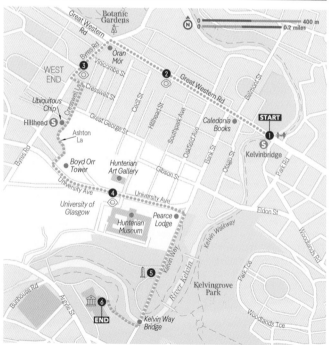

① Kelvin Bridge

Emerge from the subway and turn left across Kelvin Bridge, emblazoned with the lion rampant of the Hillhead burgh on the south side and the city coat of arms on the north. It crosses the leafy course of the River Kelvin, a tributary of the Clyde.

② Great Western Road

Continue along Great Western Rd, stopping for a browse in Caledonia Books (p141). At the corner of Byres Rd, a former church is now Oràn Mór (p138); consider its lunchtime theatre session A Play, a Pie and a Pint. Across the road stretch the Botanic Gardens (p132).

③ Student Central

Turn left down Byres Rd, gateway to the university district. Go left for Cresswell Lane with its quirky shops, and continue down Great George Lane and its cobblestoned continuation Ashton Lane, lined with lively pubs; The Ubiquitous Chip (p132) is still one of the city's best places to eat.

④ University Avenue

Take a left along University Ave and enter Glasgow University's main campus. The ugly 1960s

Boyd Orr Tower is soon replaced by more typical sandstone terraces as you climb the hill. On the left is the modern Hunterian Art Gallery (p126); on the right, you wander through the quadrangles of the university's Neo-gothic main building with its atmospheric cloister.

⑤ Lord Kelvin

Head downhill past the turreted Pearce Lodge and its elaborately carved 17th-century gateway, a relic of the university's original Old College in the East End (now demolished), and turn right into pedestrianised Kelvin Way. This leafy avenue leads through Kelvingrove Park, past a statue of Lord Kelvin.

⑥ Kelvingrove Museum & Art Gallery

Continue across Kelvin Way Bridge, built in 1912 and decorated with the city's finest collection of outdoor sculpture. There are four groups of bronzes representing *Peace and War*; *Navigation and Shipbuilding*; *Philosophy and Inspiration* and *Commerce and Industry*. The bridge makes a fitting approach to the palatial Kelvingrove Art Gallery & Museum (p120).

WALKING TOUR

Scale Woodlands Hill's heights

Woodlands Hill, rising to the east of the River Kelvin and looking across to Gilmorehill and Glasgow University, was developed in the mid-19th century to become one of the most fashionable and affluent residential areas in the city. This walk explores what is still one of Glasgow's most exclusive addresses.

START	END	LENGTH
Kelvin Bridge	Inn Deep	1½ miles; one hour

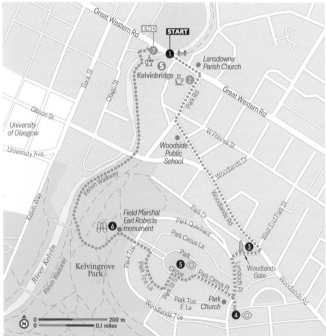

1 Kelvin Bridge

Exit the subway beside Kelvin Bridge and turn right along Great Western Rd; across the street is Lansdowne Parish Church (1863), whose 66.5m spire is one of the tallest and slimmest in the city.

2 Coffee Break

Turn right on Park Rd where the Broken Clock Cafe beckons with the promise of morning coffee. At the far end, bear left into Woodlands Rd past the imposing Victorian buildings of Woodside Public School, which now house the Stand Comedy Club and the Old Schoolhouse pub.

3 Glaswegian Humour

On the corner of Woodlands Gate stands Glasgow's weirdest monument, a bronze figure of cartoon character Lobey Dosser, his two-legged horse El Fideldo, and his arch-enemy Rank Bajin. It's a memorial to their creator, much-loved cartoonist Bud Neill, whose work appeared in Glasgow's *Evening Times* newspaper from 1949 to 1956. Head uphill and turn left into Lynedoch Place.

4 West End Spires

Ahead rise the imposing twin towers and Italian-inspired campanile of Old Trinity College (1856), originally a seminary for the education of church ministers. To the right stands the ornate Gothic tower of Park Church (1856), now orphaned – the parish church to which it was attached has been demolished.

5 Top of the Heap

The street below the tower leads to the leafy, hilltop enclave of Park Circus (1855–63), an oval terrace of exquisite Georgian townhouses modelled on Edinburgh's New Town. This was – indeed still is – one of Glasgow's most exclusive addresses, with properties selling for £1m and upwards.

6 University Panorama

Park Gate leads into the upper level of Kelvingrove Park, with a superb viewpoint across the valley of the River Kelvin to Gilmorehill, topped by the Gothic spire of the University of Glasgow. The equestrian monument is of Field Marshal Earl Roberts (1832–1914).

7 Inn Deep

Descend to the Kelvin Walkway and follow it upstream, beneath Eldon St bridge and across a footbridge to Inn Deep (p140), where riverside tables await for a well-deserved refreshment.

EXPERIENCES

Sample the Best of Scottish Cuisine

EATING OUT

MAP: **1** P118 **B2**

The original champion of locally sourced Scottish produce, the **Ubiquitous Chip** (named to poke fun at Scotland's deep-fried culinary reputation) is famed for its still-unparalleled cuisine, adding a French touch to resolutely Scottish ingredients. It was established in 1971 by Ronnie Clydesdale and rapidly became a cultural institution, frequented by writers and artists; Alasdair Gray worked on drafts of his novel *Lanark* here, and painted murals in exchange for meals – you can still see them today.

The elegant courtyard space boasts one of Glasgow's best dining experiences, while, upstairs, the brasserie offers exceptional value for money with a shorter, less expensive menu. There are two bars: the Art Deco Corner Bar and the convivial Wee Whisky Bar. And if the weather is fine there is no better spot for a drink than the Chip's rooftop terrace. All are open noon to midnight daily.

Visit a Fossilised Tropical Swamp

NATURAL FEATURE

MAP: **2** P118 **A4**

Pretty **Victoria Park**, about two miles west of Glasgow University, was created in 1887 to mark the 50th year of Queen Victoria's reign. During its construction, a road cutting exposed a magnificent series of fossilised Lepidodendron tree stumps – a remnant of the tropical swamps that once covered what is now central Scotland some 320 million years ago. In 1890 a building was constructed over the outcrop for its protection, and opened to the public as Fossil Grove (*fossilgroveglasgow.org; admission free*).

At the time of writing the building was undergoing emergency repairs and improvements, with plans to increase opening hours when the renovations are complete. Meanwhile the grove is open noon to 4pm on the third Sunday of each month from April to October.

Escape to a Peaceful Garden

GARDENS

MAP: **3** P118 **C1**

The marvellous thing about walking into Glasgow's gorgeous Botanic Gardens (*glasgowbota nicgardens.com; admission free*) is the way the traffic noise of busy Great Western Rd suddenly fades into the background. The highlight is a series of awesome Victorian glasshouses, the most impressive of which is the **Kibble Palace**, an impressive structure of wrought-iron and glass dating from 1873 – one of the largest glasshouses in Britain. Check out the herb garden, too, with its medicinal plants.

There are **self-guided trails** to follow – pick up a leaflet in the

Kibble Palace – and the verdant grounds make the perfect place for a picnic lunch. There are also organised walks and concerts in summer – have a look at the notice board near the entrance (or the website) to see what's on.

View Rarely Seen Museum Items

MUSEUM

MAP: **4** P118 **B4**

The **Kelvin Hall** (*glasgowlife.org. uk; admission free*) is an enormous sandstone palace that opened in the 1920s as one of Britain's largest exhibition centres, covering an area of six acres (2.4 hectares). It later served as a concert venue (Elton John played here in 1972), and from 1988 to 2010 it was home to the city's Museum of Transport (now moved to the Riverside Museum, p102).

Following renovations in 2016, it is today a mixed leisure and arts space. In addition to gym and sports facilities, it provides storage space for collections from the Hunterian Museum. The **Collections Showcase** and **The Avenue** – a long corridor leading off the entrance foyer – house changing displays of objects from the muse-um stores that are rarely seen. You can take a free 45-minute guided tour of the building at 10.30am on Saturday mornings; tours must be booked online in advance.

Wander the Quads of an Ancient University

HISTORIC BUILDING

MAP: **5** P118 **C3**

Founded in 1451, the University of Glasgow is the second oldest in Scotland after St Andrews, and the fourth oldest in the UK (after Oxford and Cambridge). The university was originally located in the East End near the cathedral, but moved to its current location in Gilmorehill in the 1870s. Since then the main campus has expanded across the West End between Byres Rd and the River Kelvin, but at its heart remains the imposing Gothic Revival **Gilbert Scott Building** of 1872 – named after its designer, the renowned architect George Gilbert Scott, who also designed the Albert Memorial in London. With its 85m-tall central tower, it fairly dominates the West End from its hilltop position.

You can wander freely through the elegant east and west quadrangles of the Gilbert Scott Building

---

LORD KELVIN

William Thomson, Lord Kelvin (1824–1907), was a child genius who began studying at Glasgow University at the age of 10 and went on to patent more than fifty inventions and publish more than six hundred scientific papers. One of the most eminent scientists in history, he was responsible for establishing the Kelvin scale of temperature and the Second Law of Thermodynamics, and was instrumental in achieving the first working transatlantic telegraph cable.

and the atmospheric **cloister** that links the two – a forest of Gothic columns that looks like a film set for a Harry Potter film. Afterwards, visit the Hunterian Museum (p124), housed on the upper floor of the building.

Partake of West End Park Life
PARK

Kelvingrove Park (MAP: **6** P118 D4) was laid out on the banks of the meandering River Kelvin in the 1850s as a leisure garden for the city's middle and upper classes, who were escaping from the industry, pollution and slum housing of the city centre and East End. It hosted the 1888 and 1901 International Exhibitions; the latter saw the opening of the Kelvingrove Art Gallery & Museum (p120). The park is dotted with historical monuments. The largest is the **Stewart Memorial Fountain** (MAP: **7** P118 D5), built in 1872 to commemorate Robert Stewart, the Glasgow Lord Provost (mayor) who oversaw the provision of the city's first reliable clean water supply.

The hugely popular 2000-seat **Kelvingrove Park Bandstand** (MAP: **8** P118 D4), built in 1924, has seen many memorable concerts, including gigs by Tom Jones, Van Morrison and Texas. It was renovated in 2014 and since then has hosted the annual Summer Nights at the Bandstand (*whatsonglasgow. co.uk*) festival, with 12 nights of live music in late July and early August.

Bargain-Hunting on Byres Road
SHOPPING

Byres Rd forms the backbone of the West End's bohemian quarter, a hotbed of independent shops, art galleries, fashion boutiques, antiques stores, cafes, bars and restaurants. But the most atmospheric areas are the narrow lanes that lie just off **Byres Rd**. These were formerly mews – the name given to the stables, carriage sheds and servants quarters that occupied the rear of upmarket Victorian tenement buildings – but have been converted into cute cobbled streets of quirky cottage-style businesses.

Begin in the north at **Cresswell Lane**, where you'll find De Courcy's Arcade (p141) and a idiosyncratic collection of independent shops and vintage boutiques. At the south end, continue along Great George Lane which soon becomes photogenic **Ashton Lane**, famous for its busy restaurants and bars, with tables spilling onto the street. The lane beside the Ubiquitous Chip (p132) restaurant leads back to Byres Rd; directly across the street is the entrance to **Ruthven Lane**, another hidden enclave of vintage fashion, vinyl record shops, artisan jewellery, antiques and collectables.

Dive into a West End Festival
ARTS FESTIVAL

MAP: **12** P118 G4

From its inception in 1996 until its cancellation due to the Covid pandemic in 2020, the West End Festival was Glasgow's biggest arts event. Beginning in 2023, it has been replaced by the smaller (at least, so far) but still sizeable **WestFest** (*westfest.co.uk*), with around 150 arts events in more than 60 venues across the West End encompassing music, theatre, comedy and visual art. The festival runs for the entire month of June.

Highlights include drag shows at the Kelvingrove Park Bandstand (p134), an outdoor *ceilidh* (traditional Scottish music and dancing) on the steps of Kelvingrove Art Gallery, and doors-open days when you can visit historic buildings that are usually closed to the public, such as Arlington Baths, a beautiful Victorian swimming pool and Turkish bath that is normally a members-only club.

Tour the West End's Whisky Bars

TOUR

MAP: 13 P118 **G6**

If you have trouble telling your Ardbeg from your Edradour, sign up for a tour with **Once Upon A Whisky** (*onceuponawhisky.co.uk; per person £65*). These 2½-hour guided walking tours will lead you around the West End's best whisky bars and talk you through a series of four malt whisky tastings, taking you from newbie to knowledgeable in no time. Between bars your guide will regale you with fun facts

BEST WEST END CURRIES

Glasgow's South Asian community accounts for more than 10% of the city's population; little wonder then that Glasgow's (and indeed Scotland's) favourite meal is a curry.

Mother India

MAP: 9 P118 **D6**

A stalwart among Glasgow curry houses for decades; the quality and innovation here are superb. Separate children's menu.

Mother India's Cafe

MAP: 10 P118 **C5**

The little sister of the above feels more like a pub than a restaurant but serves the same excellent curries in tapas-style portions.

Shish Mahal

MAP: 11 P118 **F3**

The legendary birthplace of chicken tikka masala has been a Glasgow institution since 1964, run by three generations of the same family.

about whisky and quirky anecdotes about the neighbourhood.

If you already know about whisky, don't miss the chance to visit the Bon Accord (*bonaccordpub. com*), one of Glasgow's finest whisky bars, with over 500 varieties on offer.

Catch a Comedy Gig at The Stand

ENTERTAINMENT

MAP: **14** P118 **F3**

The Glasgow sense of humour is legendary – the city has produced more than its fair share of comedians, from Billy Connolly, Elaine C Smith and Jerry Sadowitz to Susan Calman, Frankie Boyle, Kevin Bishop and many more. **The Stand** (*thestand.co.uk*) comedy club, set in an old school building in the West End, provides an opening for new talent in their Tuesday night open-mic spot and hosts improv sessions on the first Monday of each month. Saturday night is their signature show, a five-act special showcasing the best local comedians with the occasional big name. Book early, as Saturday nights sell out fast.

The Stand is one of the venues for the **Glasgow International Comedy Festival** (*glasgowcomedyfestival.com*), a 2½-week feast of funny that brightens up the second half of March.

Share in a Street Food Feast

EATING OUT

MAP: **15** P118 **C6**

An industrial warehouse on a West End backstreet might not sound like a great place for a night out, but Dockyard Social (*dockyard social.com*) is something else. From Friday to Sunday the warehouse contains a street food market serving a range of 'global comfort food', from burgers to bao buns, tacos to Thai, washed down with whatever

you fancy from the venue's three bars. You eat at communal tables and DJs provide the backing music. Buy tickets online (£6 per person including one drink) for a given time slot, and rock up with an appetite.

Investigate Your Scottish Ancestry

HISTORIC LIBRARY

MAP: **16** P118 **G6**

Opened in 1911 (the foundation stone was laid by the Scottish-American industrialist and philanthropist Andrew Carnegie), the **Mitchell Library** (*glasgowlife. org.uk*) is Europe's largest public reference library, holding more than a million items. The imposing Edwardian Baroque building with its distinctive copper dome is a city landmark. Its reference and lending libraries, reading rooms, public computers and cafe are freely open to the public, but the most interesting part is the opportunity for visitors to explore their Scottish ancestry – many thousands of people emigrated from Glasgow to England, North America, Australia and New Zealand in the 19th and early 20th centuries. On the fifth floor are records of births, deaths and marriages from 1855 to the present day, Church of Scotland parish registers, burial and cremation records, the Glasgow electoral records from 1857 to 1962 and the complete archives of the City of Glasgow. Staff are only too happy to help you out with your investigations.

LISTINGS

Best Places for...

€ Budget **€€** Midrange **€€€** Top End

Eating

Asian

Non Viet €€

17 D1

Stylish cafe decorated with conical *nón-lá* straw hats and bicycles, and serving authentic Vietnamese cuisine; the pho is fragrant and flavoursome. *nonviet.co.uk; 11.30am-3pm & 5-10pm Mon-Fri, noon-10pm Sat & Sun*

Hanoi Bike Shop £

18 B2

Tucked away just off Byres Rd, this upbeat spot offers creative takes on Vietnamese food, using fresh ingredients and home-made tofu. The various pho dishes are delicious. *hanoibikeshop. co.uk; noon-9pm*

Wudon €€

19 E2

Tasty sushi, fried noodles and ramen soups among other Asian dishes in a clean, contemporary setting. It's a friendly spot with helpful service. *wudon-noodlebar.co.uk; 12.30-10pm Tue-Sun*

Pickled Ginger €€

20 E6

Savour the flavours of Japan in the middle of the Finnieston strip, from sushi and sashimi to teriyaki and katsu curries, washed down with Asian-inspired cocktails. *pickledgingerfinnieston. co.uk; noon-10pm Sun-Thu, to 11pm Fri & Sat*

Cafes

Left Bank €€

21 E3

Outstanding eatery with a wide-ranging menu good for a shared meal of seasonal and local produce, with an eclectic range of influences. Great breakfasts and brunches. *theleftbank.co.uk; 10am-10pm*

Lagom Bakery €€

22 E2

The name is Swedish for 'not too much, not too little', but you may want too much of the baked delights and ice creams on offer here.

Excellent breakfast and brunch menu too. *instagram.com/lagom _bakery_eatery; 8am-5pm Mon-Sat, from 9am Sun*

University Cafe €

23 A3

It's been here since 1918, with an interior little-altered since then. Run by the fourth generation of the Italian founding family, it serves its own-recipe homemade ice cream and deep-fried Scottish comfort food. *instagram.com/ the_university_cafe1918; 10am-8pm*

Epicures €€

24 A2

Set in the leafy West End district of Hyndland, this appealing bistro has a flower-bedecked terrace and a menu of signature brunch dishes from eggs Benedict to shakshuka. *epicures.co.uk; 9am-5pm*

Brunch Club €€

25 B5

Hungover and hungry? Slept in past noon? Fear not, the Brunch Club serves all your favourite brunch dishes all day,

See p118 for map of locations

EXPLORE

WEST END

137

every day. Hair of the dog? Order the 'boozy brunch', with a bellini plus two more cocktails of your choice. No bookings. *thebrunchclub.co; 9am-5pm*

Scottish

Stravaigin

26 E3

A serious foodie's delight, with a menu constantly pushing the boundaries of originality. With a range of eating spaces across three levels, it's pleasantly casual and easygoing. *stravaigin. co.uk; noon-11pm*

Ox & Finch

27 D6

Grab a cosy booth and prepare to have your tastebuds wowed with innovative dishes drawing on French and Mediterreanean influences but focusing on quality Scottish produce. *oxandfinch. com; noon-10pm*

Number 16

28 A4

This cosy narrow space offers a short menu of quality Scottish cuisine. Innovative flavour pairings add interest but never feel pretentious. *number16.co.uk; noon-2.30pm & 5.30-9pm*

Bothy

B2 see also 18

Boasting a combo of modern design and comfy retro furnishings, this bistro blows apart the myth that Scottish food is stodgy and uninteresting, offering traditional home-style fare with a modern twist. *bothyglasgow. co.uk; noon-10pm*

Cail Bruich

29 C1

Elegant restaurant with a forage ethos that brings surprising, tangy, herbal flavours to plates that are always interesting. *cail-bruich.co.uk; 6.30-10pm Tue-Thu, noon-4.30pm & 6.30-10pm Fri & Sat*

Gannet

30 D6

This jewel of the Finnieston strip offers a cosy wood-panelled ambience and gourmet food that excels on presentation and taste backed up by an exciting wine list. *thegannetgla.com; 5.30-9.30pm Wed, noon-2pm & 5.30-9.30pm Thu-Sat*

Roastit Bubbly Jocks

31 A4

A local favourite on the main drag of Dumbarton Rd, Roastit's (the name is Scots dialect for 'roast turkey') serves

hearty Scottish comfort food with added flair. *roastitbubblyjocks.com; 5-9.30pm Wed & Thu, from 11am Fri & Sat, 11am-7pm Sun*

Gastropubs

The Finnieston

32 D6

This gastropub recalls the area's shipyard heritage with a cosy belowdecks atmosphere and nautical motifs. Excellent G&Ts and cocktails accompany a short menu of upmarket pub fare showcasing sustainable Scottish seafood. *thefinniestonbar. com; noon-10pm Mon-Sat, to 9pm Sun*

Òran Mór

33 C1

This temple to Scottish dining and drinking is a superb venue in an old church, serving high-quality bar meals in a dark, Mackintosh-inspired space. *oran-mor. co.uk; noon-10pm*

International

Six by Nico

34 D6

Enjoy a six-course tasting menu that changes every six weeks, each based around a theme: sometimes a specific national cuisine, sometimes more whimsical, like Hollywood or Childhood. *sixbynico. co.uk; noon-10pm Tue-Sun*

Butchershop Bar & Grill ●●●
35 C5

Offering several different cuts of properly aged beef, this is one of the best spots in Glasgow for a tasty, served-as-you-like-it steak. It also has a little seafood on the menu. *butchershop glasgow.com; noon-10pm Sun-Thu, to 11pm Fri & Sat*

Partick Duck Club ●●
36 A3

Away from the bustle of the Finnieston strip, this cool dining spot serves top-quality comfort food for breakfast, lunch, and dinner. *partickduckclub. co.uk; 9am-9pm*

Bay Tree ●
37 F2

Lots of vegan and vegetarian options, filling mains (mostly Middle Eastern and Greek), generous salads and a good range of hot drinks. Famous for its breakfasts (until 2pm). *thebaytreewestend.co.uk; noon-9.30pm Wed & Thu, to 10pm Fri, 10am-10pm Sat, 10am-9.30pm Sun*

Five March ●●
38 F5

Set on a quiet street on the south side of exclusive Woodlands Hill, this place takes a relaxed approach to fine food, with imaginative fusion dishes that include a good choice of vegetarian options. *fivemarch.co.uk; 5-9pm Mon-Wed, from noon Thu, noon-10pm Fri & Sat*

Gloriosa ●●●
39 C5

Luscious Mediterranean-influenced dishes – a starter of salt cod with potato, orange and fennel, followed by paccheri pasta with aubergine, tomato and marjoram – served in sophisticated surroundings. *gloriosaglasgow. com; noon-midnight*

Fish & Chips

Catch ●●
40 ¥ E3

Every neighbourhood needs a fish and chip shop, and of course the West End has a posh one – tempura prawns and banana blossom are on the menu alongside the usual haddock in batter. Sit in or take away. *catchfishandchips.co.uk; noon-9.30pm Mon-Thu, to 10.30pm Fri & Sat, 2-9.30pm Sun*

Drinking

Coffee Shops

Ottoman Coffeehouse
41 F6

A breath of fresh air away from the bland, big-name branded coffee shops, this place is like a throwback to a quieter time, with its armchairs, sofas and oriental rugs. The coffee is excellent too. *ottomancoffeehouse. co.uk; 9am-7pm Tue-Fri, from 10am Sat & Sun*

Bars

Kelvingrove Café
42 D6

A beautiful wood floor, leather banquettes, elegant fittings and chessboard tiling give this place the feeling of a timeworn local, offset by posh cocktails and solicitous table service. *kelvingrovecafe.com; 10am-1am*

Brewdog Glasgow
43 B5

Serves the delicious range of artisanal beers from the brewery of the same name. Punk IPA is refreshingly hoppy, with new releases and guest beers to explore; tasting flights mean you can try several. *brewdog.com; noon-10pm Sun-Thu, to 11pm Fri & Sat*

Brel

 B2

This Belgian bar has a conservatory dining room (with *moules frites* on the menu) so you can pretend you're sitting outdoors when it's raining, and there's an appealing beer garden for when the sun shines. *brelbar.com; noon-11pm Sun-Thu, to 1am Fri & Sat*

Hillhead Bookclub

 C1

Easygoing West End bar that's a student favourite with seriously cheap drinks, comfort food and numerous intriguing decorative touches. There's even a ping-pong table. *hillheadbookclub.co.uk; noon-midnight Mon-Fri, from 11am Sat & Sun*

Vodka Wodka

 B2

Every vodka drinker's dream, offering more varieties of the liquid fire than you could possibly sample in one sitting. Its brushed-metal bar dishes out the vodka straight and in cocktails, to students during the day and groups of mid-20s in

the evening. *vodkawodka. fun; noon-midnight*

Pubs

Jinty McGuinty's

 C2

There's something authentically Irish about this place, which has an aged wooden floor, booth seating, a literary hall of fame and a beer garden alongside it. Live music most nights. *jintys.co.uk; 11am-midnight Mon-Sat, from 12.30pm Sun*

The 78

 D6

More a comfortable lounge, The 78 offers cosy couch seating and reassuringly solid wooden tables, as well as an inviting range of ales. There's weekend DJs and occasional live music in a very welcoming atmosphere. *the78.co.uk; 4pm-1am Mon & Tue, from 2pm Wed-Fri, from noon Sat & Sun*

Inn Deep

 E2

A fabulous spot on the banks of the Kelvin; grab a craft beer and head for the outdoor tables by the riverside path. The indoor vaulted spaces beneath the bridge are characterful. *inndeep.com; noon-midnight Mon-Sat, to 11pm Sun*

Shopping

Food & Drink

Roots, Fruits & Flowers

 E2

With three separate entrances, this store combines a florist, an excellent fruit-and-vegetable vendor, plus a larger organic-produce shop and deli that includes a good bakery cafe. *rootsfruitsand flowers.com; 7.30am-6pm Mon-Sat, from 9am Sun*

George Mewes Cheese

 B3

The aromas wafting from the counter here will tempt you to buy, and helpful and friendly staff are keen to offer you samples of anything you would like to try. *georgemewescheese. co.uk; 9am-5pm Mon-Fri & Sun, to 6pm Sat*

Valhalla's Goat

52 E2

The selection of worldwide beers here, mostly of the small-producer variety, has to be seen to be believed. It also has an interesting wine selection and some tasty handmade chocs. *valhal-lasgoat.com; 11am-8pm Mon-Sat, from noon Sun*

Cottonrake Bakery

53 E2

A proper neighbourhood bakery – join the locals popping in for their morning croissants, Danish pastries and sour-dough loaves, and linger to enjoy a cappuccino while you admire the works of Glasgow artists adorning the walls. *cottonrake.com; 8am-5pm Mon-Sat, 9am-4pm Sun*

Books & Comics

Caledonia Books

54 E2

The favourite shop of Stuart Murdoch (of the band Belle and Sebastian) and just what a secondhand bookshop should be, with a wide range of intriguing volumes on slightly chaotic shelves. *caledoniabooks.co.uk; noon-6pm Tue-Sat*

City Centre Comics

55 B2

Part of the Ruthven Lane complex, with a good range of back issues, both recent and from past decades. Though the shop looks small, the selection is huge. *citycentrecomics.com;*

11am-4pm Tue, Thu & Fri, 10am-5pm Wed & Sat, noon-4pm Sun

Art & Design

De Courcy's Arcade

56 C2

This bijou two-level arcade has a selection of tiny boutiques offering vintage clothing, art, homewares and more. The opening hours of individual shops can vary. *facebook.com/decourcysarcade; 10am-5.30pm Mon-Sat, noon-5pm Sun*

Hidden Lane

 D6

Concealed down a passageway off the Finnieston strip, these back alleys house a colourful mix of arty shops and studios worth investigating. *thehidden-laneglasgow.com; hours vary, mainly 11am-5pm Mon-Sat*

Papyrus

58 C1

This innovative West End store is a fine place to choose gifts for folks back home, with everything from jewellery to homewares. *papy-rusgifts.co.uk; 9am-6pm Mon-Sat, 10.30am-5pm Sun*

Studio

59 B2

At the far end of the Ruthven Lane complex, this arcade has several shops specialising in antiques, design and retro items. *artscraftsglasgow.co.uk; 11am-5.30pm Mon-Sat, noon-5pm Sun*

Fashion

Pink Poodle

60 C2

A colourful boutique stocking a wide range of designer clothing for women, with lots of unique items in a variety of styles. Not particularly cheap, but always an interesting browse. *pink poodleboutique.co.uk; 10am-5.30pm Mon-Sat, noon-5pm Sun*

Duds Vintage Clothing

61 C1

Riffle your fingers through the well-stocked racks in this Aladdin's Cave of retro chic in search of the perfect pair of Levi 501s or that elusive Iron Maiden T-shirt. *instagram.com/duds_vintage; noon-5pm*

Glasgow Toolkit

Family Travel.................................144

Accommodation.................................145

Food, Drink & Nightlife.................................146

LGBTIQ+ Travel.................................148

Health & Safe Travel.................................149

Responsible Travel.................................150

Accessible Travel.................................152

Nuts & Bolts.................................153

Index.................................154

Central Station (p46)

KENSOFTTH/SHUTTERSTOCK ©

Family Travel

Glasgow is easy to visit with children, with an simple-to-use public transport system and friendly locals. The city boasts excellent kid-focused attractions and most restaurants are welcoming to family groups.

Green Spaces for Kids

Glasgow isn't known as the 'Dear Green Place' for nothing: there are loads of public parks, often next door to the major sights, where kids can run wild in safety. Check out **Kelvingrove Park** (pictured below; p134) in the West End, **Glasgow Green** (p66) in the East End and **Pollok Country Park** (p98) in the Southside.

GLASGOW WITH KIDS

This website run by a young mum living in the city is a brilliant resource for finding out about places to go and things to do as a family. **Scan the QR code:**

Eating Out

Glasgow restaurants generally cater very well for families, but be aware that a few pubs, even if they serve meals, may not admit children – it all depends on the conditions of their licence. In family-friendly pubs (look for a kids' menu), accompanied children are no problem. If you're not sure whether the pub is family-friendly, just ask the bartender.

Pushing Prams

Most of Glasgow's streets are buggy-friendly, but in some parts of the centre and the West End the hills are very steep.

Public Transport

Children under five travel free on public transport, and those aged five to 15 pay a reduced fare.

Admission Fees

Most paid attractions offer a discounted admission fee for children under 16. However, the majority of Glasgow's big-ticket sights are completely free for both kids and adults.

FROM LEFT: AC MANLEY/SHUTTERSTOCK ©, SKULLY/SHUTTERSTOCK ©

Accommodation

Glasgow offers a wide range of places to stay, from budget-friendly hostels and cosy B&Bs to boutique hotels and five-star luxury options.

Where to stay if you love...

Architecture, art and shopping

Merchant City (p71) Mostly midrange with a few budget choices, close to City Halls for classical concerts, the Gallery of Modern Art, classic Victorian architecture and the best shopping streets.

Bars, live bands and films

Central Glasgow (p37) Raucous nightlife along Bath St and western Sauchiehall St can be noisy, but there's a good choice of budget options, chains, and top-end aparthotels, with quieter upmarket options near Blythswood Square.

Markets and medieval history

East End (p55) There aren't too many accommodation options in the East End, mostly budget places concentrated along High St, which are handy for the cathedral and the Barras, plus a handful of B&Bs east of the Necropolis.

Parks and gardens

Southside (p95) The sprawling Southside is mostly green, with rental flats and B&Bs in leafy suburbs close to the magnificent Burrell Collection and Mackintosh's House for an Art Lover (pictured below).

HOW MUCH FOR A NIGHT IN A

Budget chain hotel
£70

Midrange chain hotel **£120**

Luxury boutique hotel **£210**

OUR PICK

★

We love to stay in the...

West End (p117)
This is where you'll find the best mix of major sights, places to eat and bars to drink in, all wrapped up in one of the city's liveliest and most attractive neighbourhoods. Choose from gorgeous Airbnb tenement flats in quiet back streets to luxury hotels to Scotland's poshest youth hostel.

145

Food, Drink & Nightlife

Allergies & Intolerances

Servers will often ask about allergies or intolerances, and many menus now list items containing gluten, nuts, meat or dairy.

Vegetarian restaurants Commonly found in neighbourhoods all over Glasgow. Vegetarian options are on almost every menu.

Vegan restaurants Almost as prevalent as vegetarian restaurants; there's usually one vegan option on most menus.

Gluten-free restaurants Becoming more common, offering no cross-contamination in the kitchen.

AT THE CHIPPIE
The chippie (fish and chip shop) is a stalwart of Glasgow's fast-food culture, but here you ask for a 'fish supper', not 'fish and chips'.

THE FINNIESTON STRIP

In many ways, the West End is the powerhouse of Glasgow's food scene, with the area around Byres Rd a hub of quality eating, and the Finnieston 'Strip' (Argyle St around its junction with Kelvingrove St) the heartland of fashionable eateries. Great Western Rd and Gibson St also offer excellent choices.

 ### Glasgow Spice

Glasgow is the curry capital of Scotland – one in ten of the population is of South Asian descent, and the city boasts some of the best Indian, Pakistani and Bangladeshi cuisine in the country. Try **Mother India** (p135), **Shish Mahal** (p135) or **Ranjit's Kitchen** (p114).

HOW TO...

Pay the Bill

Usually, you won't get your bill at a restaurant until you get your server's attention to ask for it.

Splitting the bill It's common among groups of friends to split the bill evenly. It's polite for those who've had extra dishes and more expensive wine to offer to pay more.

Tipping It's courteous to leave a 10% tip at a restaurant. A service charge of 10% to 12% may be automatically included on the bill, especially for larger groups. It's not necessary to tip in a pub unless there's been outstanding service. Drinks are paid for at the bar when you order, unless you leave your card and open a tab.

PRICE RANGES

The following price ranges refer to the average cost of a main course.

£ less than £12
££ £12–22
£££ more than £22

OPENING HOURS

Cafes 8am to 5pm
Pubs 11am to 11pm
Restaurants noon to 10pm
Fast-food joints 11am to midnight

Going Out

Glaswegians love a night out, and there are drinking establishments to suit all sorts.

Pubs The city's pubs are gloriously friendly places and you're sure to have some entertaining blethers (chats) with locals when you pop into one. They're typically open between 11am and 11pm, with some classic Victorian pubs still sporting 19th-century mahogany and brass interiors.

Cocktail bars Clever mixologists serve up imaginative menus of craft cocktails in stylish surroundings, but the atmosphere is never pretentious; they're usually open between 5pm and 1am. Among the best are Kelvingrove Café and Stravaigin in the West End, the Spiritualist in the Merchant City, and Platform in the city centre.

Clubs After a cocktail or three people head for a club around 11pm and dance into the wee hours, until 3am or 4am at weekends. Top clubs include Sub Club, New World, Buff Club and the Polo Lounge.

HOW MUCH FOR A

Sandwich £3–8

Pint of beer £3–6

Burger £6–12

Meal at a high-end restaurant £80+

Meal for two at an average restaurant with wine £30–60

Barista coffee £3–5

Street food dish £5–12

Fish supper £9–15

LGBTIQ+ Travellers

Glasgow's hospitality and friendliness extends to its LGBTIQ+ scene, where the locals give a warm welcome to visitors.

The Pink Triangle

Glasgow's gay scene is the biggest in Scotland, and is focused on a handful of streets in the Merchant City area. Known as the Pink Triangle, the main zone stretches from the junction of Wilson St and Virginia St to the south end of John St, and includes pubs, bars, clubs and shops, with a low-key daytime vibe morphing into happy party nights with a lot less attitude (bouncers aside) than is the norm. A handful of other venues are scattered across Central Glasgow.

The streets of the district come alive with Glasgow's annual Pride march, and there's also a carnival atmosphere during July's Merchant City Festival, when street art, live music and dance promise a load of fun.

PRIDE

Glasgow's Pride (*glasgowspride.org*) is a major event in the city, drawing a crowd of 50,000 marchers. The date is variable, but it's usually held on a Saturday in late July.

OUR PICKS

Queer Bookshops

The Southside's **Category Is Books** is one of only eight dedicated queer bookshops in the UK, with a fine selection of gay literature and history. **Calton Books** in the East End, self-described as 'the best wee radical bookshop in the world', also has a strong LGBTIQ+ section.

LGBT HEALTH & WELLBEING

LGBT Health & Wellbeing offers free information and advice for the LGBTIQ+ community in Scotland.

Resources

● **Somewhere: For Us** (*somewhereforus.org*) A print magazine, website and podcast made by and for Scotland's LGBTIQ+ community, focusing on the arts, culture and news. ● **Pink News** (*thepinknews.com*) London-based but covers events in Scotland.

Health & Safe Travel

Glasgow is a relatively safe and healthy city to visit, but petty crime does happen. Here are some tips on staying safe.

TAP WATER

Glasgow's tap water is among the best in the world, coming from Loch Katrine in the Highlands. Ask for tap water in restaurants to avoid paying for the bottled stuff. Refill stations are becoming more common; check *yourwateryourlife. co.uk* for your nearest Top Up Tap.

Theft

Pickpocketing and bag- or phone-snatching are the main crimes, with Central and Queen St train stations and Buchanan St subway station the hotspots. Don't leave phones or handbags lying around in bars or restaurants or have them sticking out of your back pocket. Put valuables in the main section of a backpack, and wear it on your front in busy areas. Don't leave bags unattended.

Health Insurance

Glasgow offers free healthcare for UK citizens. Foreign nationals should ensure they have insurance.

Snow & Ice

Snow and ice are not uncommon in Glasgow during the winter months. Pavements will be gritted, turning them into a slush-fest; even so, much of the transport infrastructure still gets delayed after heavy snow. Expect journey times to be longer in icy conditions, and plan to leave earlier than normal.

QUICK INFO

Security
Bike theft is common so always lock yours, ideally with two locks.

Privacy
Glaswegians prefer you ask before taking their photo. Avoid taking photos of kids.

Marijuana
Medical-use cannabis is legal with documentation; recreational use is illegal.

--- SECTARIANISM ---

The football rivalry between Rangers and Celtic in Glasgow is a serious one; don't get involved in pub banter unless you understand the context.

149

Responsible Travel

Follow these tips to leave a lighter footprint, support local businesses and have a positive impact on communities.

Go Meatless

Glasgow has a growing number of vegan and vegetarian restaurants, and almost all menus have an option for non-meat eaters. Choose a day to go meatless, and help reduce deforestation and greenhouse gas emissions.

FROM LEFT: MARAZE/SHUTTERSTOCK ©, JIM BYRNE SCOTLAND/SHUTTERSTOCK ©, HOME BIRD/ALAMY STOCK PHOTO ©

Low Emission Zone

Glasgow introduced a Low Emission Zone (*glasgow.gov.uk/LEZ*) in 2023, covering Central Glasgow and the Merchant City inside the M8 road and north of the river. You can enter your vehicle's registration number at *lowemissionzones.scot* to see whether it complies with the regulations. Blue Badge holders, historic vehicles, motorcycles and mopeds are exempt; unlike in London, you cannot pay to enter an LEZ in Scotland.

OUR PICK
★
Too Good to Go

The Too Good to Go scheme (*toogoodtogo. com*) tackles 'plate waste' in restaurants, making it normal to take leftovers home after a meal. Just ask for a 'doggie bag'.

Resources

- **cyclestreets.net** For planning bike-friendly routes.
- **travelinescotland.com** Essential tool for using public transport.

--- **ELECTRIFYING PUBLIC TRANSPORT** ---

Glasgow has a fleet of more than 200 electric buses that save 4.4 million litres of diesel and 10,000 tonnes of CO_2 per year. They join the already electrified subway and suburban rail network.

Secondhand Shopping

Glasgow is a veritable paradise for lovers of secondhand goods, preloved clothing and vintage fashion. Visit the East End's legendary weekend flea market at **the Barras** (pictured elow right; p66), a noisy, colourful compendium of all things repurposed and upcycled, with a taste of authentic Glasgow culture thrown in.

Seekers of vintage fashion, antiques and bric-a-brac will find plenty of temptation in the trendy **Byres Road** (p134) area of the West End – check out places like **De Courcy's Arcade** (p141), **Hidden Lane** (p141) and **Ruthven Lane**. Over in the Merchant City, **Mr Ben** (p93) is one of the city's best vintage shops; south of the river, head for the colourful **Park Lane Market** (p115) and the **Glad Rags** (p115) emporium of thrift.

BEER FROM BREAD

Glasgow's pioneering Jaw Brew microbrewery has embraced the circular economy model by taking leftover bread rolls from the local Aulds bakery and using them as the base for their award-winning Hardtack beer.

Climate Change & Travel

It's impossible to ignore the impact we have when travelling and Lonely Planet urges all travellers to engage with their travel carbon footprint, which will mainly come from air travel. While there often isn't an alternative, travellers can look to minimise the number of flights they take, opt for newer aircrafts and use cleaner ground transport, such as trains. One proposed solution – purchasing carbon offsets – unfortunately does not cancel out the impact of individual flights. While most destinations will depend on air travel for the foreseeable future, for now, pursuing ground-based travel where possible is the best course of action.

The **UN carbon footprint calculator** shows how flying impacts a household's emissions.

The **ICAO's Carbon Emissions Calculator** allows visitors to analyse the CO2 generated by point-to-point journeys.

Accessible Travel

Public Transport

City buses have steps that can be lowered to street level and there is a dedicated wheelchair space on lower decks; it's shared with buggies and can be full when you board, but wheelchair users have priority. ScotRail stations and trains have lifts and ramps, but the subway is not accessible.

Accessible Streets

Central Glasgow has numerous pedestrianised areas, such as Buchanan St and Argyle St, which are ideal for wheelchair users. General pavement quality along main thoroughfares is fine, but watch out for the steep hills north of Sauchiehall St.

GUIDE DOGS

The UK's Equalities Act requires museums, hotels and transport to allow access to guide dogs (or face prosecution). This law doesn't include emotional support dogs, but some venues allow them.

Accommodation

Glasgow has many accessible accommodation options. Modern hotels can feature beds and baths designed with wheelchairs in mind, and lowered wardrobes and bedside tables, plus wide doorways. Enquire before you book.

OUR PICK

As Scotland's most popular free attraction, **Kelvingrove Art Gallery & Museum** (p120) is well-equipped for less able visitors. The car park has disabled parking bays and step-free access to the building; inside, there's a reception desk with staff trained in British Sign Language, plus accessible toilets and lifts. The galleries have been designed with wheelchair and buggy access in mind; interactive exhibits are at wheelchair height and most have induction loops and subtitles.

--- **OFF-LIMITS SUBWAY** ---

Because of its small coaches and lack of lifts, wheelchairs are not permitted on the subway unless they can fold up. The same goes for prams and pushchairs.

Resources

● Visit Glasgow (*visitglasgow.org.uk*; scan the QR code) Tips on navigating the city in a wheelchair.

● AccessAble (*accessable.co.uk*; scan the QR code) Great resource for accessible venues.

⬡ Nuts & Bolts

🕐 Opening Hours
Expect seasonal changes and different hours by location (city centre or suburbs). No set closing time for clubs.

Banks 9am–5pm Monday to Friday, to 3pm Saturday

Post offices 9am–5.30pm Monday to Friday, to 12.30pm Saturday

Pubs & bars 11am–11pm or noon–midnight, some until 1am Friday and Saturday

Restaurants noon–10pm

Museums & galleries 10am–5pm, from 11am Friday and Sunday

Shops 9am–6pm Monday to Saturday, some until 8pm Thursday, 11am–5pm Sunday

Airports, shopping centres, cafes and many restaurants offer free Wi-Fi.

QUICK INFO
Time zone GMT/UTC (+1 during summer)
Country code +44
City code 141
Emergency number 999 or 112
City population 632,350

ELECTRICITY
230V/50Hz

📅 Public Holidays
Although bank holidays are general public holidays in the rest of the UK, in Scotland they only apply to banks and some other commercial offices.

New Year 1 and 2 January

Good Friday March or April

Easter Monday March or April

May Day First Monday in May

Spring Holiday Last Monday in May

Glasgow Fair Saturday before the 3rd Monday in July

Autumn Holiday Last Monday in September

Christmas Day 25 December

Boxing Day 26 December

Weights & Measures
Glasgow officially uses the metric system (grams, litres etc), but pubs still sell beer by the pint (568ml), and grocery stores sell milk in one-, two- and four-pint containers. Distances on road signs are still in miles (1 mile is equal to 1.6km).

Index

Sights **000**   Map pages *000*

See also separate subindexes for:
- ✴ **Eating** p156
- 🍷 **Drinking** p157
- 🛍 **Shopping** p157

A

accessible travel 152
accommodation 24, 27, 145, 152
activities 14
air travel 28, 151
ancestry 136
architecture 17
area codes 153
arriving 28
art galleries 13 , 60, 106
Art Laundrette 45
Ashton Lane Hogmanay Street Party 26

B

bagpipes 49, 66-7
Barras 66
bathrooms 25
bicycle travel, *see* cycling
boat trips 110, 112
Botanic Gardens 132
bouldering 112
Boyd Orr Tower 129
breweries 52, 67, 69, 139-40, 151
Britannia Panopticon 88
budget 25, 147
Burrell Collection 98-101
bus travel 29
business hours 147
Byres Rd 134

C

car travel
   low emission zone 150
Celtic Connections 89
Celtic FC 68, *see also* football
Central Glasgow 37-53, *38-9*
   drinking 47, 50, 52-3
   entertainment 46-50
   food 51-2
   itineraries 42-5, *42, 44*
   shopping 53
   sights 40-1

transport 37
   walks 42-5, *42, 44*
Centre for Architecture and Design 46
Centre for Contemporary Arts 50
children, travel with 19, 144
cinemas 48, 50
Citizens Theatre 113
City Centre Mural Trail 87
City Chambers 74-7
City Halls 87
City Sightseeing Glasgow 88
climate 26
clubs 8, 49, 52, 92, 147
Clyde Walkway 112
Clydeside Distillery 111-12
comedy 135, 136
costs 25, 31, 147
Cuningar Loop 112
currency 25
cycling 30, 112, 150
   history 103

D

dangers, *see* safety
Dear Green Place, the 67
design 17
disabilities, travellers with 152
distilleries 111-12, *see also* whisky
Dockyard Social 136
drinking & nightlife 8-9, 146,
   see also clubs, *individual neighbourhoods*, Drinking *subindex*
drinks, *see* breweries, distilleries, whisky
driving, *see* car travel
drugs 149
Duke of Wellington statue 86

E

East End 55-69, *56*

drinking 69
   entertainment 66-68
   food 69
   itineraries 62-5, *62, 64*
   shopping 65-6
   sights 57-61
   transport 55
   walks 62-5, *62, 64*
electricity 153
emergencies 153
entertainment 10-11, *see also* comedy, live music, *individual neighbourhoods*, Entertainment *subindex*
etiquette 24
events, *see* festivals & events

F

family travel 19, 144
festivals & events 18, 26-7, 48
films 48, 50
food 6-7, *see also individual neighbourhoods*, Eating *subindex*
   allergies & intolerances 146
   curry 146
football 27, 68, 111, *see also* Celtic FC, Queen's Park FC, Rangers FC
Frank, Hannah 32
free experiences 19
Friends of Glasgow Royal Infirmary Museum 67-8

G

galleries 13
Gallery of Modern Art 81
gay travellers 148
gardens, *see* parks & gardens
George Square 80
Gilbert Scott Building 133
Glasgow Boys 123
Glasgow Cathedral 57-9

Glasgow Central Tours 46
Glasgow Cross 65
Glasgow Film Theatre 48
Glasgow Green 66
Glasgow International Comedy
     Festival 136
Glasgow Music City Tours 89
Glasgow Necropolis 61
Glasgow Police Museum 86
Glasgow School of Art 47
Glasgow Science Centre 104-5
Glasgow's Museum of Piping
     49
Glasgow Subway 32
Glasgow Tower 104
Glenlee 103
Gorbals St Bridge 32
Gorbals, The 32
Govan Stones 110

H

Hampden Park 111
health 149
highlights 6-19
history 16
     ancient 110
     domestic 47-8
     medical 67-8, 124-5
     shipbuilding 111
     trade 88
holidays 153
Holmwood House 110
Homeless Jesus 32
House for an Art Lover 106-7
Hunterian Art Gallery 126-7
Hunterian Museum 126-7
Hutcheson's Hall 83

I

itineraries 20-3, *see also
     individual neighbourhoods*

K

Kelvin, Lord 125, 129, 133
Kelvin Hall 133
Kelvin Walkway 131
**Kelvingrove Art Gallery &
     Museum 120-3**
Kelvingrove Park 134
Kibble Palace 132

L

LGBTIQ+ travellers 148
Lighthouse, The 46

live music 8, 10, 50, 87, 88-9
Lord Kelvin 125, 129, 133
Lynch, Benny 32

M

Macdonald, Margaret 107
Mackintosh at the Willow 40-1
Mackintosh, Charles Rennie
     47-8, 106-7, 123
Mackintosh House 126-7
**Mackintosh Interpretation
     Centre 46**
Mackintosh Queen's Cross 48
markets 66, 87-8, 115
medical services, 153
Merchant City 71, *72*
     drinking 91
     entertainment 86-9
     food 90
     itineraries 82-5, *82, 84*
     murals 89
     shopping 92
     sights 86
     transport 71
     walks 82-5, *82, 84*
Merchant Square 87
Mitchell Library 136
money 25, 146-7
motorcycle travel 150
Museum of Piping 49
museums 12, *see also individual
     sights*
music, *see* bagpipes, live music

N

Nelson's Monument 66
nightclubs, *see* clubs, drinking
     & nightlife
nightlife, *see* drinking & nightlife,
     Drinking *subindex*
North Woodside 49-50

O

Old Firm, the, *see* football
opening hours 147, 153
outdoors activities 14-15

P

pantomime 27
parks & gardens 66, 112, 132-3,
     134, 144, 145
Pavilion Theatre 46
Pinkerton, Allan 32
Planetarium 105

planning
     booking 24
     clothes 24
     tips 24
police 153
Provand's Lordship 66
PS *Waverley* 112
public holidays 153
pubs 147

Q

Queen's Park FC 111, *see also*
     football

R

Rangers FC 68, *see also* football
religion 60
responsible travel 150
River Clyde 95
River Kelvin 130
Riverside Museum 102-3
Reid Building 45

S

safety 149
Scotland Street School 113
Scottish Events Campus 113
Scottish Football Museum 111
Seaforce Powerboats 110
Sharmanka Kinetic Theatre 78
shipbuilding 111
shopping 151, *see also* markets,
     individual neighbourhoods,
     Shopping *subindex*
soccer, *see* football
Southside & the Clyde 95-115,
     96-7
     drinking 115
     entertainment 110-13
     food 114
     itineraries 108-9, *108*
     shopping 115
     sights 98-107
     transport 95
     walks 108-9, *108*
St Andrew in the Square 65
St Mungo 59
**St Mungo Museum of Religious
     Life & Art 60**
Stand, The 136
subway 29, 32
**Summer Nights at the
     Bandstand 27**
surprises 32

INDEX

T

taxis 30
Tenement House 47-8
Tennent's Brewery 67
Thomson, Alexander 'Greek' 110
time 25
tipping 25
tobacco lords 88
toilets 25
top experiences 6-19
tours 46, 80, 88, 89, 135, *see also* walks
train travel 28, 30
transport 29, 31
TRNSMT 27

U

Universtiy of Glasgow 131

V

Victoria Park 132

W

walks
    Central Glasgow 42-5, *42, 44*
    East End 62-5, *62, 64*
    Merchant City 82-5, *82, 84*
    Southside & the Clyde 108-9, *108*
    West End 127-31, *128, 130*
weather 26, 149
weights & measures 153
West End 117-41, *118-19*
    drinking 139-40
    entertainment 132-6
    food 137-9
    shopping 140-1
    sights 120-7
    tours, 135
    transport 117
    walks 128-31, *128, 130*
WestFest 135
whisky 11-12, 135
World Pipe Band Championships 66

🍴 Eating

A
Art Lover's Cafe 114

B
Bar 91 90
Bar Soba 51
Bay Tree 139
Bothy 138
Brooklyn Cafe 114
Brunch Club 137
Brutti Compadres 90
Butchershop Bar & Grill 139

C
Café Gandolfi 90
Cafe Strange Brew 115
Cail Bruich 138
Catch 139
Celentano's 69
Chawp Pet Noi 114
Copperbox Coffee 69
Corona Bar & Kitchen 114

D
Dakhin 91

E
Epicures 137
Errol's Hot Pizza 114

F
Finnieston, The 138
Five March 139

G
Gamba 51
Gannet 138
Glaschu 90
Gloriosa 139
Gusto & Relish 115

H
Hanoi Bike Shop 137

L
Laboratorio Espresso 51
Lagom Bakery 137

Left Bank 137
Little Hoi An 114
Loon Fung 51

M
Mono 90
Mother India 135

N
Non Viet 137
Number 16 138

O
Òran Mór 138
Oro 114
Ox & Finch 138

P
Paesano Pizza 91
Partick Duck Club 139
Pickled Ginger 137

R
Ranjit's Kitchen 114
Red Onion 51
Riverhill Coffee Bar 51
Roastit Bubbly Jocks 138

S
Salt & Vinegar 114
Singl-end 51
Six by Nico 138
Soulsa Bar & Kitchen 90
Spanish Butcher 90
Spitfire Espresso 90
St Luke's & the Winged Ox 69
Stravaigin 138

U
Ubiquitous Chip 132
University Cafe 137

V
Van Winkle 69

W
Whistler on the Green 69
Willow Tea Rooms 51
Wilson Street Pantry 90
Wudon 137

Drinking

78, The 140

A

Arches 49
Artà 91
AXM 92

B

Babbity Bowster 91
Bar Gandolfi 91
Blackfriars of Bell St 91
Bramble 115
Brel 140
Brewdog Glasgow 139
BrewDog Glasgow Merchant City 91
Buff Club 52
Butterfly and the Pig 53

C

Cafe Strange Brew 115
Cathouse Rock Club 52
Classic Grand 52
Clutha & Victoria Bar 115
Corinthian Club 86, 91

D

Delmonica's 92
Drum & Monkey 53
Drygate 69

F

Flying Duck 52

G

Glad Cafe 115

H

Hillhead Bookclub 140
Horse Shoe Bar, The 53

I

Inn Deep 140

J

Jinty McGuinty's 140

K

Katie's Bar 92
Kelvingrove Café 139

M

MacSorley's 53

N

Nice N Sleazy 52

O

Ottoman Coffeehouse 139

P

Platform 52
Polo Lounge 92
Pot Still, The 52

R

Red Sky Bar 115
Rum Shack 115

S

Salon de Luxe 41
Saracen Head 69
Shilling Brewing Co 52
Slouch Bar 52
Speakeasy 92
Spiritualist 91
Sub Club 52

U

Underground, The 92

V

Vodka Wodka 140

W

Waterloo Bar 53
West on the Green 69

 Shopping

A

Adventure 1 53
Argyll Arcade 92

B

Barras 66
Buchanan Galleries 53

C

Caledonia Books 141
Celtic Store 53
City Centre Comics 141
Cottonrake Bakery 141

D

De Courcy's Arcade 141
Duds Vintage Clothing 141

G

George Mewes Cheese 140
Glad Rags Thrift 115
Glasgow Print Studio 93

H

Hidden Lane 141

L

Love Music 53
Luke & Jack 93

M

Monorail 93
Mr Ben 93

P

Papyrus 141
Park Lane Market 115
Pink Poodle 141
Princes Square 92

R

Record Fayre 93
Roots, Fruits & Flowers 140

S

Slanj Kilts 53
St Enoch Centre 92
Stephen O'Neil Art 115
Street Level Photoworks 93
Studio 141

V

Valhalla's Goat 140

Send Us Your Feedback

We love to hear from travellers – your comments help make our books better. We read every word, and we guarantee that your feedback goes straight to the authors. Visit lonelyplanet.com/contact to submit your updates and suggestions.

Note: We may edit, reproduce and incorporate your comments in Lonely Planet products such as guidebooks, websites and digital products, so let us know if you are happy to have your name acknowledged. For a copy of our privacy policy visit lonelyplanet.com/legal.

Acknowledgements

Cover photograph: Glasgow Science Centre. Alan Copson/ AWL Images ©

Back photograph: Glasgow Cathedral. coleong/Getty Images ©

THIS BOOK

Destination Editor
Amy Lynch

Cartographers
Julie Sheridan,
Mark Griffiths

Production Editor
Andrew Owen

Book Designer
Dermot Hegarty

Assisting Editors
Hannah Cartmel,
Kate Mathews

Cover Researcher
Kat Marsh

Thanks to
Ronan Abayawickrem
Sofie Andersen
Alison Killilea
Ailbhe MacMahon

Although the authors and Lonely Planet have taken all reasonable care in preparing this book, we make no warranty about the accuracy or completeness of its content and, to the maximum extent permitted, disclaim all liability arising from its use.

Published by Lonely Planet Global Limited
CRN 554153
3rd edition – June 2025
ISBN 978 1 83758 354 6
© Lonely Planet 2025
Photographs © as indicated 2025
10 9 8 7 6 5 4 3 2 1
Printed in Malaysia